# Quotable Jazz

by
**Marshall Bowden**

D1563392

Caricatures
by
Mike Rooth

Sound And Vision

# TABLE OF CONTENTS

## III. MUSICIANS SPEAKING FREELY

## IV. STYLES, PEOPLE, AND PLACES

## V. SOME OF THE GREATS

## VI. FINAL THOUGHTS

# Introduction

Jazz music attracts a lot of unique individuals, be they musicians, fans, collectors, critics, hipsters, or lonely beat poets. This motley cast of characters has a tendency to discuss, converse, confer, and argue about the smallest details of the music and the lives of the men and women who make it. So, for example, if one writes about a great solo John Coltrane played at a specific gig on a specific date, there is sure to be someone who will send in a lengthy diatribe on the timetables of Philadelphia trains and the alignment of Jupiter's sixth moon which proves, beyond any reasonable doubt, that Coltrane could not possibly have played the gig in question on the date in question.

Beyond the "statistics"—who played what where and when and on which recording— there is always the question: to which school of jazz does a particular cat hold allegiance? For some, gutbucket trombone and soaring clarinet signals the only true sound of jazz, while for others it is the swing of the dance band that is the real McCoy (Tyner). Then there are the boppers, who dismiss all these as moldy figs and advise their elders to get hep. The West Coast cats want the boppers to cool out, the hard boppers want to get some funk in the bucket, the free jazzers just want to blow, and the fusion kids want to turn the volume up, up, UP! Then you have new traditionalists, third streamers, world fusionists, jam bands, and others all vying for a place in the jazz tradition. In short, the word "jazz" may mean both more and less than it ever has, and its current state may well resemble an anarchist's dream. Personally, I truly enjoy jazz in all of its forms from ragtime right up to free jazz, fusion, and some of today's electronica/jazz experiments. To those who seek to limit jazz to a particular style or period of time I say: a pox upon ye! For that reason I have sought to include representatives of all styles and periods within these covers.

The volume you hold in your hands right now does not purport to offer any type of comprehensive history or overview of jazz. It is not even a comprehensive collection of quotations, though I believe it is the largest and most inclusive collection of quotes exclusively about jazz music and musicians currently to be found in print. What *Quotable Jazz* is, I hope, is a representation of the enormous variety and individuality of the minds and thoughts of those who have had, and continue to have, enormous influence on the music. It demonstrates that there are always arguments to be had, always different ways of defining the same problem. Some of the quotes in these pages are hilarious, others rather sad, still others funny because of who said them or when or where they were said. Hopefully you'll get a feel for the minds behind some of the best music and writing in jazz, as well as a sense of some of the issues that have come up during its one hundred year history.

The topics covered include many familiar to most jazz musicians and fans: the definition of jazz and of swinging, drugs, drink, sex, the gig, the audience, other musicians, race, the many kinds of jazz. Maybe you'll be surprised at the things some of these folks have said, maybe not. But I can guarantee that there is enough ammunition here to keep jazz aficionados talking for weeks, even months.

I've done my best to keep the quotes pithy and the explanations short, but there are the unavoidable references to the circumstances under which a quote was delivered or the person who it is about. I thought this better than interrupting the natural flow of the speaker's language. In some cases, you may read the quote, then the attribution, then go back and reread the quote with a new appreciation. As Miles Davis said, "I'll play it and tell you what it is later." I've also tried very hard not to take quotes out of context and to preserve the speaker or writer's original meaning, though this is difficult in certain cases. Still, I don't think I've seriously misrepresented anyone here, and that was certainly never my intention, though the juxtapositions of quotes are sometimes deliberately meant to provoke thought even though in some cases the quotes are separated in time by fifty or more years.

Another caveat: the language in some of these quotations is, to put it mildly, rather strong. Certain expletives abound. This is certainly not unusual to anyone who has read the jazz literature or spent time around musicians, but for those who have not, be warned. Of course, should you find that the language in this book is not nearly strong enough, by all means seek out the four volumes of Library of Congress recordings by Jelly Roll Morton available on Rounder Records CDs. I guarantee it'll make whatever you see here look mild by comparison.

Finally, a bit of a plea from the soapbox. It's a cliché, but jazz music really is an American art form, possibly the only one, certainly the most celebrated. Musicians develop their own individual voices by playing a great deal, and playing for a live audience is the best possible experience. Sadly, though, jazz clubs are in short supply these days and those that do exist are often not financially successful. In addition, jazz festivals are more and more becoming the preserve of the famous artist, so the opportunities for future generations of musicians to develop are shrinking. The always forward-looking U.S. government is not funding music education or the arts the way that any truly advanced society should. Please do whatever you can to encourage young people to listen to music besides what the giant entertainment conglomerates are feeding them, help them learn to play an instrument, support the arts in your community wherever in the world you are. Who knows? Maybe someday they'll compile a book like this one.

Marshall Bowden
www.jazzitude.com
Chicago, IL
September, 2002

# A Few Acknowledgements

My gratitude for my parents' support over the years is enormous. I want to say thanks for giving me a love of the arts and an insatiable curiosity, all the piano & saxophone lessons, for sticking with me and giving me a push when it was needed. My Dad passed away before I completed this book, but he knew I was working on it and had seen some of the content as well as the cover. I know he was proud and I wish he were here to see it finished. Hey, Mom, I did it!

Thanks and much love to Elizabeth, who has been there for me for more years than I care to remember, and who has supported me and believed in me even when I didn't believe in myself. You—be cool!

Thanks to Geoff Savage at Sound And Vision Books for initiating this project and giving me the opportunity to do it. Thanks also to Mike Rooth for his fantastic caricatures of jazz artists.

In addition, I'd like to say greetings and thanks to Michael Ricci at *All About Jazz* for his generous advice and support in creating my *Jazzitude* website. Thanks also to Sarah Zupko, Michael Stephens, and Barbara Flaska at *PopMatters* for their general support.

A quick hello to the folks at Treehouse Animal Foundation in Chicago. Love to the best cats in the world: Melvina the wondercat who is no longer with us, Benjamin, the love muffin, PowWow, the snickerdoodle, and Rita Mae, the cupcake.

Now, let's get on with it, man!

## DEDICATION

For my parents
Sam and Margaret Bowden
And for
Elizabeth Seelig

# I. SOME DEFINITIONS

WHAT IS JAZZ? TAKE ONE: MUSICIAN'S DEFINITIONS
## Conversations With Myself

*Musicians tend to give two kinds of answers when asked to explain what jazz is. The first kind is overly intellectual and verbose, but earnest. The second is a jive answer. Curiously, these types of flippant answers—short, sweet, and to the point—often end up explaining or illuminating a lot more about the music and the person who makes it than the first type of answer.*

Jazz is music made by and for people who have chosen to feel good *in spite of* conditions.

**Johnny Griffin**

What I came back to is that jazz is a music to be played and not to be intellectualized on.

**Gerry Mulligan**

Jazz is the folk music of the machine age.

**Paul Whiteman**

Well, the word jazz bothers me. It bothers me because, as long as I've been publicly identified with it, I've made less money and had more trouble than when I wasn't.

**Charles Mingus**

Jazz is what you can play before you're all screwed up; the other is what happens after you're screwed up.

**Lennie Tristano**

Oh, jazz and love are the hardest things to describe from rationale.

**Mel Torme**

# Quotable Jazz

People who use terms like the "Chicagoans" or "New Orleans Style"—I despise that stuff...I get so disgusted with the idea that you have to be from one particular part of the country to be able to play good jazz.

**Pee Wee Russell**

Jazz tickles your muscles, symphonies stretch your soul.

**Paul Whiteman**

[Jazz] went from the classics to ragtime to Dixieland to swing to bebop to cool jazz . . . But it's always jazz. You can put a new dress on her, a new hat, but no matter what kind of clothes you put on her, she's the same old broad.

**Lionel Hampton**

As it enters the ear, does it come in like broken glass or does it come in like honey?

**Eddie Condon**

Roaming through the jungle of "oohs" and "ahs," searching for a more agreeable noise, I live a life of primitivity with the mind of a child and an unquenchable thirst for sharps and flats.

**Duke Ellington**

We Americans use such denigrating words about this music: Jazz or Bebop. These are not high-class words. But it's street music so you have to use the vernacular.

**Phil Woods**

I don't care too much about music. What I like is sounds.

**Dizzy Gillespie**

Jazz has got to have *that thing*. You have to be born with it. You can't even buy it. If you could buy it, they'd have it at the next Newport festival.

**Miles Davis**

If you have to ask what jazz is, you'll never know.

**Louis Armstrong**

It's almost like I don't want to even try to define it.  I really don't.  I just want to play.
**John Scofield**

WHAT IS JAZZ? TAKE TWO: CRITICS' AND FANS' DEFINITIONS:
## Birth of the Cool
*Critics and fans tend to be more intellectual and earnest in trying to get at the core of jazz, but they often end up being funny without really meaning to. Those who are critical of jazz (qualifying neither as critic in the best sense nor as fans) often make the sharpest, most humorous remarks.*

Jazz may be a thrilling communion with the primitive soul; or it may be an ear-splitting bore.
**Winthrop Sargeant**

Jazz is to real music what the caricature is to the portrait.
**Dr. Frank Damrosch, Director of the Institute of Musical Art, 1924**

Jazz music is the delirium tremens of syncopation.
**Walter Kingsley**

The term mainstream jazz probably means less now than it ever has.  Jazz is, now, itself and whatever else you can get away with.
**Stanley Crouch**

Jazz music is an intensified feeling of nonchalance.
**Francoise Sagan**

Someone once wrote that the sound of surprise is jazz, and if there's any one thing that we must try to get used to in this world, it's surprise and the unexpected.
**Warren G. Bennis**

Boxing is like jazz. The better it is, the less people appreciate it.
**George Foreman**

The chief trouble with jazz is that there is not enough of it; some of it we have to listen to twice.
**Don Herold**

WHAT IS JAZZ? TAKE THREE: SOCIAL CRITICISM:
## I Get Along Without You Very Well
*Then there is the type of "definition" or commentary that is completely critical of jazz music, the musicians who play it, and, often, the effects of that music upon society. Often these comments thinly veil a distinctly racist agenda. Yikes!!*

A wave of vulgar, filthy and suggestive music has inundated the land. Nothing but ragtime prevails, and the cakewalk with its obscene posturings, its lewd gestures.
**The Musical Courier, 1899**

Jazz originally was the accompaniment of the voodoo dancer, stimulating the half-crazed barbarian to the vilest deeds.
**Anne Shaw Faulkner, 1921**

It seems to me monstrous that anyone should believe that the jazz rhythm expresses America. Jazz rhythm expresses the primitive savage.
**Isadora Duncan**

Jazz: Music invented by demons for the torture of imbeciles.
**Henry Jackson Vandyke, Jr., U.S. clergyman, educator & author**

Giving jazz the Congressional seal of approval is a little like making Huck Finn an honorary Boy Scout.
**Melvin Maddocks**

I do not think jazz is leading America anywhere.
**Booth Tarkington, 1924**

By and large, jazz has always been like the kind of a man you wouldn't want your daughter to associate with.
**Duke Ellington**

No other folk music in the world's history has ever induced among normal people such curious psychopathic aberrations as the desire to wear a zoot suit, smoke hashish, or jabber cryptic phrases of "jive" language.
**Winthrop Sargeant**

The word jazz in its progress toward respectability has meant first sex, then dancing, then music. It is associated with a state of nervous stimulation...
**F. Scott Fitzgerald**

JAZZ LINGO:
# Jivin' with Jack the Bellboy
*Jazz musicians have always spoken their own language, partially as a way of setting themselves apart from the rest of the world and partly because they tend to think in more colorful linguistic terms than most folks. Our language would be dull without some of these contributions from the hepcats.*

Nobody knows what a square is—it's just that nobody wants to *be* one.
**Duke Ellington**

The technical name for what we play is 'revived archaic jazz'. We have been accused of cleaning the music up, but we simply play it with right notes and chords.
**Chris Barber**

Cab Calloway Jive:
*viper*: a dope smoker
*drape*: a suit of clothes
*gate*: a "cat"
*hip*: wise or sophisticated
*Jeff*: a square
 **From *Cab Calloway's Cat-ologue: A Hepster's Dictionary***

Lester Youngisms:
*Needle dancer*: heroin addict
*Did you wear a hat?*: Did you have sex?

17

*Pound cake*: a hot woman
*Bing and Bob*: the police
*Can Madame burn?*: Can your wife cook?
*Grays*: white people
*No eyes*: disapproval

How are we to know that a Dracula is a key-pounding pianist who lifts his hands up to his face, or that a bass fiddle is the doghouse, or that schmaltz musicians are four-button suit guys and long underwear boys?
**New York City, U.S. public relief program on jazz musicians' argot**

## II. THE JAZZ LIFE

THE JAZZ LIFE, SOME GENERAL OBSERVATIONS
*Dealing with the law, competing with other musicians, waiting for a break, playing in clubs all night or in the studio all day—these are just a few of the concerns of jazz musicians.*

A jazz musician have to be a working class of man, out in the open all the time, healthy and strong. That's what's wrong today; these new guys haven't got the force. They don't *like* to play all night; they don't think they *can* play unless they're loaded.
**Johnny St. Cyr**

If you couldn't blow a man down with your horn, at least you could use it to hit him alongside the head.
**Mutt Carey**

I used to stand out on the sidewalk listening to the opposition. Eventually I'd walk in and try to cut them. If they wouldn't invite me up to the bandstand, I'd get my trumpet out by the side of the stand and blow at them from there.
**Roy Eldridge**

Pops, breaks come to cats in this racket only once in a while and I guess I must have been asleep when mine came.

### Joe "King" Oliver

I'm just an average guy. When I say 'average guy,' I mean I like...just simple things. I like to go out to a movie now and then, to a musical or some sort of play; I saw *Phantom of the Opera* and I saw *Cats*.

### McCoy Tyner

That's something I've learned: it can be a bobby or it can be a policeman or it can be a gendarme, but I don't care what language it is—a cop is nothing but a cop, and he's bound to do things his way.

### Sidney Bechet

I am not a person who will go back to the hotel room right after the gig and go right to bed. I am pretty curious, and I am always afraid I'm going to miss something.

### Diana Krall

In the main, jazz musicians are home-loving, television-watching, newspaper-reading innocents who dislike night clubs, late hours, buses, and all other discomforts their jobs force on them.

### Whitney Balliett, *The New Yorker*

### Blues:
## Kind of Blue

*The blues are a huge part of the language of jazz, kind of the way Latin is the basis of English...you may not speak it, but it's in there somewhere.*

Blues means what milk does to a baby.

### Alberta Hunter

You can't rehearse a blues, darlin'."
**Joe Williams**

Some people take a ballad and sing it real slow and say it's the blues. Don't believe 'em.
**Alberta Hunter**

I merely took the energy it takes to pout and wrote some blues.
**Duke Ellington**

When you play the blues, (the whores) will call you sweet names and buy you drinks and give you tips.
**Louis Armstrong, recalling his teenage years in New Orleans**

I do not claim any of the creation of the blues, although I have written many of them even before Mr. (W.C.) Handy had any blues published. I had heard them when I was knee-high to a duck.
**Jelly Roll Morton**

Blues is to jazz what yeast is to bread—without it, it's flat.
**Carmen McRae**

There's always this confusion between sociology and music. When you try to teach students, you can't teach them sociology. You have to teach them something about music. I can't stand in front of a class and say, "Well, man, I want you to go home and stand on a corner with a chicken wing, and then come back and put some barbecue sauce on it, and come back next week, and then you will be able to play some blues."
**Wynton Marsalis**

Drinking:

# Straight, No Chaser

*There's nothing funny about alcoholism and some really talented musicians (Bix Biederbecke, Fats Waller) have died early as a result of their battle with the bottle. Nonetheless, some of the antics and anecdotes related by these heavy drinkers and their observers seem humorous because they are funny stories or because of the speaker's own insight into their difficulties with alcohol.*

I was playing organ at a silent movie house in Harlem and they'd be showing some death scene on the screen, likely as not I'd grab a bottle and start swingin' out on "Squeeze Me" or "Royal Garden Blues". The managers complained, but heck, they couldn't stop me!

**Fats Waller**

You should see some of those old fellows down in New Orleans I grew up with. My, they're old! Shuffling along, can't remember nothin'. Couldn't play a chorus to save their life. Whiskey got to some of them. Whiskey heads are all dead! Bunk is still here!

**Bunk Johnson**

When I first joined the band, in the forties, he would have a fifth of Scotch in the bus, after the job, and he'd drink some of it. Later, it got to be all of it.

**Milt Bernhart on Stan Kenton**

After we finished a job he would always say "Thank you. Thank you very much for the gig." Then he would go get drunk.

**Zoot Sims on Stan Kenton**

I can say one thing: no woman ever drove me to drink!

**Teddy Wilson**

(Fats Waller) kept two bottles of gin on a table during the rehearsals. One was for himself...The other bottle was the "encourager" as he called it. When one of the band excelled in an improvisational section, (he) would stop the rehearsal, pour him a healthy shot of gin, and the two of them would toast each other.

**Maurice Waller**

I think I had it in the back of my mind that I wanted to sound like a dry martini.

**Paul Desmond**

## Quotable Jazz

I figured out that I drunk enough whiskey to float the battleships of the world and all the submarines.
**Wild Bill Davison**

Milk is bad for you.  Ask Pat Boone.
**Frank Sinatra**

Jesus Christ, my boys don't even start vomiting till eleven.
**Tommy Dorsey, on being told his band
had to arrive on a film set at 8 AM**

Everybody that's not high on the next set gets a ten-dollar fine.  We can't play sober.
**Stuff Smith**

I never even realized that there was a similarity or relationship between drugs and alcohol.  I switched from drugs to alcohol and I became a rather functional person...
**Stan Getz**

We don't flat our fifths, we drink 'em.
**Eddie Condon**

I had a lot of cats who could play good, but they couldn't hold their whiskey.
**Roy Eldridge**

We all have bad habits. Bird liked whiskey. I eat ice cream excessively.
**Gigi Gryce**

I'm probably the best guy to tell about those swing days because I'm probably the only one who was ever sober.
**Johnny Guarnieri**

I used to drink to forget...and I did!
**Anita O'Day**

Warm vodka. There's nothing worse.
**Frank Sinatra**

DRUGS:
## Jack, I'm Mellow

*As with alcohol, drugs are not a funny topic when you are talking about lives and careers that were sent spinning off track or ruined. Some of these quotes point out the ridiculousness of pretending drug abuse doesn't exist in the jazz world while others offer insight into the addicts themselves.*

Examine a list of all the musicians who have run afoul of the law on this charge (narcotics) between, say, 1945 and the present! The roster is neither small nor unrepresentative. It makes, in fact, an abridged jazz *Who's Who*.
**Gary Kramer**

I can't believe I'm still alive.
**Jaco Pastorious, 1985**

If my habit hadn't been illegal and expensive I might have been all right.
**Chet Baker**

A dope addict, from what I noticed by watching a lot of different cats, who I used to light up with but got so carried away, they felt that they could get a much bigger kick by jabbing themselves in the ass with a needle—heroin, cocaine, etc. or some other ungodly shit, which would not ever faze a man like myself, who's always had a sane mind from the day he was born.
**Louis Armstrong**

# Quotable Jazz

I go to this heart specialist, you know, give him a hundred dollars for the relief of my heart. He treats me, don't do no good; my heart is still messed up. I go to this ulcer man, give him seventy-five dollars to cool my ulcers out; it don't do no good. There's a little cat in a dark alley around the corner. I give him five dollars for a bag of shit; my ulcer's gone, my heart trouble gone, everything gone, all my ailments gone.
**Charlie Parker**

Bird died trying to kick his habit. He tried to kick it the wrong way, by drinking whiskey. The whiskey is the thing that killed him. The heroin was preserving him...
**Art Blakey**

I don't think anyone every accomplished or proved anything by saying "You're involved in narcotics. Get out of my band."
**Woody Herman**

I know a lot of strung-out dudes who couldn't play shit; they should have just got high and enjoyed themselves and forgot about playing.
**Hampton Hawes**

I was personally sent to Chinatown many times with a sealed note and a small amount of money and would bring back several cards of hop. There was no slipping and dodging. All you had to do was walk in to be served.
**Jelly Roll Morton**

An old friend told me recently when he was coming to New York, Max Roach told him one thing: 'Stay away from Charlie Parker, and stay away from Sonny Rollins.'
**Sonny Rollins on his days as a drug abuser**

I feel that if this government that can protect the Persian Gulf and be down in Nicaragua and do all these things, they

24

certainly can stop heroin and cocaine from coming into this country. So somebody's making some money.
**Jackie McLean**

A FEW REMARKS ON THE "MUSICIANS' TOUCHSTONE",
# Marijuana:

I can handle the juice, but that stuff sent me outa my nut!
**Stan Kenton**

I smoked (marijuana) a long time. And I found out something. First place, it's a thousand times better than whiskey. It's an assistant, a friend, a nice cheap drink if you want to call it that.
**Louis Armstrong**

Joe Bushkin was the first cat to lay a roach on me, when I was about nineteen years old. That's when I went to whiskey immediately after that.
**Frank Sinatra**

When we left L.A., going on the road, I had a dozen Prince Albert cans of Mexican pot. Every night at intermission Pops (Louis Armstrong) and I would go out and smoke. After a week, he didn't bring his shit anymore...I said "Damn, Pops, I notice you don't bring out that New Orleans Golden Leaf." He said, "Man, that's like bringing hamburger to a banquet."
**Dexter Gordon**

There was this idea that if you smoked a joint, you would turn into a dead jazz musician. And you know, we did smoke a joint or two and all we turned into was hippies, which was bad enough, but it wasn't a dead jazz musician.
**P.J. O'Rourke**

Question: Hey, Frankie, you got any grass on you?
Frank Sinatra: Yeah, pal, I got plenty of grass. It's at home—on my lawn.

Well, I bet I'm higher than any of you.
**Stan Getz after being revived from a drug overdose**

MUSICIANS, WOMEN, AND SEX:
## Dancing In the Dark

*Jazz musicians were once the musical stars of their day, much as pop stars are today, and they had the same opportunities when it came to winning and bedding the opposite sex. Groupies, prostitutes, chorus girls, and society ladies were all available to jazz musicians as they traveled across the country playing in one town after another. Since men and women often worked together in a jazz setting, that could lead to some interesting situations as well.*

One girl follows ballplayers
her sister, sailors seeks
but *these* chicks
are something else—
they're musician freaks!
**Ira Gitler**

He always had five or six girls. He had them all in different rooms in the same hotel, and one night they were even all sitting at the table in front of the bandstand while he played. And each of them thought that she was with him.
**Bill Crow on Stan Getz**

Charlie Barnet liked drinking and smoking pot, and he loved the opposite sex. Every time he went to dinner at night he would propose to the waitress!
**Charles Colin**

I like the girls to match the upholstery of the car.
**Charlie Barnet**

There was one place with a big area of houses of ill repute and he came to work one night with one of the young ladies from one of the houses. For the next three or four nights he had a

lady come up on stage and introduced her as Mrs. Charlie Barnet.
**Billy May on Charlie Barnet**

Sometimes fashion models go around with guys who are scuffling—for a while. But usually they end up marrying some cat with a factory. This is the way the world ends, not with a whim but a banker.
**Paul Desmond**

When looking *for* a woman it always helps to find a woman who is also looking.
**Frank Sinatra**

I ain't got no free fucks to give away.
**Miles Davis to a female fan**

In the early years, when we had to take gigs—any gig—to keep going, it was always good to have a dame around who could bring in a few bucks.
**Dannie Richmond**

If I have girlfriends, they don't listen to what I'm playing. They don't care.
**Wynton Marsalis**

As time went on, it became easy to deal with questions from the audience with humor and frankness. Question: "How do you like working with men?" Answer: "I *love* it!" Question: "Does sex enter into your playing at all?" Answer: "You're darn right—especially if you're going with the drummer!"
**Marian McPartland**

For years I've nursed a secret desire to spend the Fourth of July in a double hammock with a swingin' redheaded broad. But I could never find me a double hammock.
**Frank Sinatra**

Talking 'bout wild and woolly! There were two thousand

registered girls (prostitutes) and must have been ten thousand unregistered. And all crazy about clarinet-blowers!
**Alphonse Picou**

...A lot of these kids are young so they don't know about foreplay yet, you know? I'd sort of like to ask them, when we're getting more abstract, and people are like 'C'mon!...play a groove or "Chubb Sub"', or whatever. I feel like saying, "Hey man, what's up? Is this how you are with your woman?" you know. You don't take the time to sit back. You gotta learn about foreplay.
**John Medeski**

There's always chicks that'll hang around bands and look at who's handsome and who's a soloist. If a guy knows how to give some chick the eye from the bandstand, he can end up with that chick.
**Mel Lewis**

The times I've come closest to quitting the band are the times I've been the horniest. Fortunately, that hasn't been too often.
**Mike Jamieson**

What I miss most about the road is, I really enjoyed making love to a different woman every night.
**Art Pepper**

Honey, you are just wasting your time. Don't you know musicians get it for free?
**Fred Carter to a hustling hooker**

ATTIRE:
## Goodbye Pork Pie Hat
*From the zoot suits of the swing era to the berets and glasses of the boppers to the even more casual attire often sported by musicians today, wardrobe and grooming has always been an interesting part of the jazz life.*

I came dressed as I would in Hollywood, in a pair of corduroys, a sweatshirt and loafers with probably no socks, and he said 'Where are you going, fishing?' I said 'No, I'm coming to rehearsal', and he replied 'Go home and put a suit and tie on, this is New York.'
**Jimmy Maxwell on Benny Goodman**

Now a trademark, that tuft of hair cushions my mouthpiece and is quite useful to me as a player; at least I've always thought it allowed me to play more effectively.  Girls like my goatee too...
**Dizzy Gillespie**

Order YOUR leopard skin jacket as worn by Dizzy Gillespie— Now! Just $39.50!
**Fox Brothers ad for Dizzy Gillespie "bebop clothes"**

You may have holes in your shoes, but don't let people out front know it.  Shine the tops.
**Earl Hines**

I think one of the reasons I'm popular again is because I'm wearing a tie. You have to be different.
**Tony Bennett**

This all came of a conversation I had with (John) Steinbeck once when we were standing in a men's room somewhere. Steinbeck asked me why I didn't play the banjo any more and I told him that went out with high-button shoes.
**Eddie Condon**

I was unfashionable before anyone knew who I was.
**Paul Desmond**

Tommy Dorsey would walk up to you if you had a tuxedo on and make sure you didn't have on white socks.
**Louis Bellson**

You know, jazz musicians didn't have to look good.
**Archie Shepp**

Because I'm going to *work!*
**Art Blakey on why he wore overalls to a gig**

Jazz Fans:
## A Love Supreme

*Jazz fans are a peculiar lot. They know all the recordings, who played what when and where, and the intimate details of a musician's life. Though the musicians have something of a love/hate relationship with these aficionados and hipsters they do generally appreciate the attention.*

Some people enjoy listening to jazz because somebody told them they should.
**Duke Ellington**

A teenager once said to him 'This is sixth-grade jazz!' 'Yeah" he answered, 'because the average American has a sixth-grade education, so thank you, I'm reaching them.'
**Sun Ra**

An audience is like a dame; If it ain't sincere, it's endville.
**Frank Sinatra**

I can't understand these guys who just have to have your autograph. I asked one of them 'What do you do when you get home, take it out and look at it?'
**Artie Shaw**

The best reaction I ever got? It might not sound like the best, but the first time I went to Europe with Herbie (Mann), a guy in Berlin rushed down the aisle during my solo and started pounding on the stage, screaming 'THIS IS NOT JAZZ! THIS IS NOT JAZZ! THIS IS NOT JAZZ!' At least I reached him..."
**Sonny Sharrock**

Our basic audience begins with creaking elderly types of twenty-three and above.
**Paul Desmond**

The only reason they're out there is to see me fall into the damn orchestra pit.
**Billie Holiday**

There's more bad music in jazz than any other form. Maybe that's because the audience doesn't really know what's happening.
**Pat Metheny**

Like baseball fans, jazz fans know who played where and with whom and to what effect; they talk a rarefied language and drop the names of clarinetists and percussionists as baseball fans do the names of long-forgotten (except by them) shortstops and spitballers. Their retention of detail is prodigious.
**Russell Lynes**

As long as there's one surviving musician left in town I don't know why anyone would waste their time talking to me.
**Jazz historian Bill Russell**

Is that so? Well, who's got more fans than Santa Claus?
**Coleman Hawkins on being told the reason an 8-year-old
girl wanted his autograph was because she thought he was
Santa Claus**

In the Age of Indifference, of bland Ivy and Jivey Leaguers on the make, jazz fans all, according to the Gospel of *Playboy*, to care deeply is archaic. Moldy.
**Studs Terkel**

A Fig—A traditionalist; a cat for whom jazz sort of ended with the swing era. For him Mulligan's a stew, Parker a coat, and yes, sir, he remembers Paul Desmond. Wasn't he a cowboy actor in the movies?
**Elliot Horne**

A Moldy Fig—The swing era was avant-garde stuff for this guy. He spells jazz "J-A-S-S" and reminisces passionately on jugs, washboards and riverboats. His record collection reeks of formaldehyde and the musician he digs must be dead for quite some time.
**Elliot Horne**

I hope we left you with something to put under your pillows.
**Dexter Gordon**

I know people who have everything I've ever breathed on.
**Woody Herman**

Hawk, I heard that record you made with Sonny Rollins. Don't ever do it again!
**Anonymous fan to Coleman Hawkins**

SELLING OUT:
## Thinkin' One Thing and Doin' Another
*The old Catch-22: musicians often complain, on the one hand, that they don't get their due economically or in terms of fame. On the other hand, any jazzer who becomes too popular and famous is looked upon with scorn and suspicion. How commercial is too commercial?*

Art is dangerous. It is one of the attractions: when it ceases to be dangerous you don't want it.
**Duke Ellington**

You know, if they can get on television and sell Playtex girdles and tell you about midriff bulge and all that, they damn

sure can sell some music if they want to. They say, 'Jazz is too hard to sell.' They've sold the Maharishi Yoga and Ravi Shankar playing sitars and everything. They can sell anything and make it packageable, make it commercial.
**Lee Morgan**

The more mediocre your music is, the more accessible it is to a larger number of people in the United States. That's where the market is. You're not selling to a bunch of jazz esthetes in Europe. You're selling to Americans, who really hate music and love entertainment
**Frank Zappa**

He said, "Well, is this what you're going to do with the rest of your life? Are you going to start wearing sequined suits and get your hair curled up and have a couple of lip operations?"
**Branford Marsalis on his brother, Wynton's, reaction to his playing with pop musician Sting**

I can definitely recognize greed. I know when a man is playing for money. And, good gracious, there's plenty of that going on right now!
**Coleman Hawkins**

I would rather play Chiquita Banana and have my swimming pool than play Bach and starve.
**Xavier Cugat**

Commercialism is not a bad word because it's what the American market is all about. It's what *America's* about. And when you sign with a record company *they* expect you to sell some records. You don't sign with them and say 'Now don't expect me to sell any records.' They'd think you're crazy.
**Ramsey Lewis**

Why do you judge me as a musician, John? All I'm interested in is making money.
**Glenn Miller to critic John Hammond**

## Quotable Jazz

I think Quincy Jones is a drag. I really do. Quincy was in a position to be a real leader in jazz, but he sold out so fast it was funny—for a while, until you found you weren't laughing.
**Thad Jones**

I think that which sells the best *is* the best.
**Donald Byrd**

If Charlie Parker were alive today, somebody would try to cut a disco single with him and try to get him to sell three million.
**Ben Sidran**

If an artist makes a bad LP, he'll always tell you afterward "They *made* me do that."
**Les McCann**

I have to put something out that is going to be saleable, and not just to a select jazz audience either. Some may call it prostitution; I still call it music.
**Billy Cobham**

People aren't making music out of the basic need to make music anymore. There are a lot of other reasons.
**John Medeski**

Want to hear me play jazz? —Pay me. Give me a million dollars and I'll make the greatest jazz record you ever heard, 'cause that's what I'd lose by playing it.
**George Benson**

There's such a cynicism about the phrase "I laughed all the way to the bank." It's as though money is what you're doing, rather than playing music. If you're playing a money game, why not get into banking?
**Artie Shaw**

CRITICS:
# Dance of the Infidels

*Let's face it; no one likes a bad review. Sometimes critics say the most incredible things, and part of the humor of criticism is seeing some of what was said that turned out to be completely goofy. Here, we take a critical look at critics.*

If everyone liked what I did, I probably wouldn't be playing anything of depth.
**Joshua Redman**

Critics have their purposes, and they're supposed to do what they do, but sometimes they get a little carried away with what they think someone should have done, rather than concerning themselves with what they did.
**Duke Ellington**

Because of (early jazz writers') lack of understanding of the mechanics of music, they thought there *weren't* any mechanics. It was the "they all can sing, they all have rhythm" syndrome. If that was the case, why was there only one Louis Armstrong?
**Wynton Marsalis**

I have to object to the musical nonsense currently being peddled in the name of jazz by John Coltrane and his acolyte, Eric Dolphy.
**Critic John Tynan**

Our problem is that we have replaced reality with bullshit. Anything can pass for art.
**Wynton Marsalis**

They always ask the same questions. Where was I born? When did I start singing? Who have I worked with? I don't understand why they can't just talk to me without all that question bit.
**Sarah Vaughan on the Jazz press**

What you want to know? Where I was born, and all that? You can get it all from any record album. But if you're a writer, you come downstairs and *listen* when I play the next set. Then you go and write your article.
**Coleman Hawkins to a reporter**

Damn it, when I'm bombastic, I have my reasons. I want to be bombastic—Take it or leave it.
**Dave Brubeck**

We're very rough on our own in Canada.
**Oscar Peterson**

Every guy who would compare me to Coltrane, I would compare his writing to Hemingway, compare his writing to Faulkner. I'd even tell them that. "Say, man, I was comparing your work to Faulkner. Man, you've really got a way to go."
**Branford Marsalis**

You know, I think we tend to say, "It's bad", rather than, "I don't like it."
**George Shearing**

Opinions are like assholes... everyone's got one.
**Art Blakey (probably quoting from an unknown source)**

One critic described what I was doing as "atonal stride." That's not bad.
**Sun Ra**

They think we just roll out of bed and play the D-major scale.
**Ray Brown**

I firmly believe that most writers, not all writers, they don't know where our inspiration comes from; they don't know what we are really doing. So yeah, most of them write out of their ass, but I realize that so I don't get that affected by it.
**Christian McBride**

You know, I'd never make a good critic. I just like to relax and enjoy music, but when it comes to criticizing, I'm afraid to hurt people's feelings.
**Peggy Lee**

Doesn't that fool know that I recorded that tune because I *like* it?
**Cecil Taylor on a criticism of his choice of material**

His idea of giving a musician a hint is to hit him in the face with a shovel.
**Jazz writer Otis Ferguson on critic John Hammond**

The best qualification for a jazzist is to have no knowledge of music and no musical ability beyond that of making noises either on piano, or clarinet, or cornet, or trap drum.
***The Performer*, 1919**
**(reviewing a performance of the Original Dixieland Jazz Band)**

...it was obvious even from the start that many jazz writers either do not know their subject, only care about one style (while still feeling free to write about areas that they despise), seem to put themselves on an equal level (or even higher) than the creators, or are more concerned with musicians' personalities (and judge them accordingly) than trying to understand their music.
**Jazz Writer Scott Yanow**

So if the critics haven't got everyone scared with a lot of high-flown technical talk and Jack Kerouac hasn't got everyone impressed with the beauties of numbness and hipness for hipness' sake, maybe we could launch a little enthusiasm and restore fun to its rightful place in jazz.
**Gerry Mulligan**

Critics are supposed to be people in a position to tell what is of value and what is not, and, hopefully, at the time it first appears. If they are consistently mistaken, what is their value?
**Amiri Baraka (Leroi Jones)**

How could you not be influenced by reading the same idiocies in ten different jazz journals?
**Boris Vian**

Jazz is probably the only art form whose existence depends on resistance to theories....If someone is an expert on jazz, you can be pretty sure he/she is not a vital jazz musician....
**Keith Jarrett**

The critic's simple soul needs to discover genius; that's why fat old Hughes Panaissie makes a fool of himself ten times a year by declaring ten times a year, "Whatshisname is incontrovertibly the greatest".
**Boris Vian**

He rounds it all off by asking if jazz and classical music can't get together. I should say this happened about ten years ago. The problem now is to get them apart.
**Philip Larkin**

I'm a musician, and just as the critics are sometimes hard on me, I'm hard on the critics.
**Oscar Peterson**

To me, there's only two kinds of music, good and bad. If I like it it's good, and if I don't like it, it's bad.
**Harry James**

MAKING A LIVING:
## Easy Living
*Making a living playing jazz has never been easy. Musicians comment on their lot and their attempts to make ends meet and put food on the table.*

You want to know what I was taught by all those jazz musicians I grew up around? There is no price to pay for life except to live it. And if someone wants to make you pay a price for how you live, fuck 'em.

**Wynton Marsalis**

Of course, my folks never had the idea they wanted a musician in the family. They always had it in their minds that a musician was a tramp, trying to duck work, with the exception of the French Opera House players which they patronized.

**Jelly Roll Morton**

I did never want to be successful. I want to be the only thing I could be without anybody stopping me in America—that is, to be a failure.

**Sun Ra**

It seems that in this country, you're expected to be a specialist. People get used to you in a certain role in life, and they don't like you to step out of it. In other countries, particularly the Latin countries, it doesn't surprise anyone when a man is an attorney and a jazz musician, or a playwright and a painter.

**Gerry Mulligan**

I'm fortunate that I'm making a living at it now because I'm not equipped to do anything else.

**Sonny Rollins**

You know what used to happen during the Depression? We used to play a lot of jobs and didn't get paid.

**Coleman Hawkins**

If Hawk don't like the bread, he won't take the gig. And he don't know no word but *thousand dollars*!

**Roy Eldridge on Coleman Hawkins**

I'm not interested any more in going down in history. I want to eat.

**Dizzy Gillespie**

## Quotable Jazz

I used to make the Chicago Wrigley Theatre amateur hour, on Thanksgiving, and I used to win a turkey for my family. I was a sure turkey-getter.

**Andrew Hill**

Although they paid me well in Disneyland, nobody ever listened to me.

**Judy Carmichael**

There's very few things I do in life that I do for commercial reasons. That's why I'm a poor jazz musician.

**Sonny Rollins**

The organ is the favorite instrument of Fats' heart; and the piano only of his stomach.

**Ashton Stevens, critic for the *Chicago American***

I think I would tell just about any young player, "Enjoy what you do, but don't really count on making a living at doing this".

**Art Pepper**

I don't care who likes it or buys it. Because if you use that criterion, Mozart would have never written *Don Giovanni*, Charlie Parker never would have played anything but swing music.

**Branford Marsalis**

Someday we may have as many followers as the harpsichord.

**Eddie Condon after the financial failures
of his early jazz guitar concerts**

Who told people that artists aren't supposed to feed their families beans and greens?

**Charles Mingus**

I've never really concentrated on building a so-called career. I suppose I should. Maybe I will, if it's not too late.

**Carla Bley**

While you've read the preceding paragraphs, Gerry Mulligan has recorded with three different groups for two labels.
**Downbeat Magazine**

ON THE ROAD:
## A Night In Tunisia
*If there's one thing all musicians agree on, it's that life on the road isn't easy. Many musicians tour constantly in order to make a living, and in the swing era, big bands were always in demand at dances and theatres across the country. Love it or hate it, the road is part of the life of the jazz musician.*

Tonight...one time only...Stan Kenton and his Orchestra, Featuring the Lovely Kai Winding
**Marquee at Seattle Civic Auditorium**

I spent a lot of time playing in miserable places that were not a lot of fun. Somebody once said it is character building and I was like 'My character is just fine.'
**Diana Krall**

I wonder what an agent would do if he had to travel with the band he's booking.
**Mary Lou Williams**

It did me in and I was in my early 20s then.
**Singer Chris Connor on road life**

There are more towns in America that I have only seen after dark than I would care to think about.
**Benny Goodman**

Sometimes when we're flying or in the hotel, I might run over songs, or in the bathroom.
**Ella Fitzgerald**

Life on the road is murder. It's as though life begins and ends when you have your horn in your mouth.
**Gerry Mulligan**

The fact that we've stayed on the road is not due to any help from the record companies or the airline companies. The big record outfits are too busy promoting their rock superstars, and as for airlines—well, that's my pet peeve.

**Phil Woods**

I don't get paid to play—I get paid to travel and for that "living out of a suitcase" thing. I feel very fortunate that I can do this.

**Diana Krall**

We drove 500 miles between gigs and would be fired by the time we did our soundcheck.

**Chris Wood**

I joined Count Basie's band to make a little money and see the world. For almost two years I didn't see anything but the inside of a Blue Goose bus, and I never got to send home a quarter.

**Billie Holiday**

The bus gets to stinking of dirty clothes, sweat and booze and cigarette smoke, and the guys have their shoes off and everybody's wearing their socks for two and three days, because we don't always have a chance to get them washed.

**Mel Lewis**

THE CLUB SCENE:
# Birdland

*The jazz club: a crowded, noisy, smoky joint where folks are drinking, talking, eating, pinching the waitress, and generally doing everything but listening to the music. Some musicians prefer to play in these settings; others like the concert stage more. Here are a few scenes from a night at the club.*

Most customers, by the time the musicians reach the second set, are to some extent inebriated. They don't care what you play anyway.
**Charles Mingus**

I knew there was an audience for jazz, but they were a little tired of standing up at the bar on Fifty-second Street and nursing a beer through a whole set for a buck or a buck and a half.
**Jazz impresario Monte Kay**

I'm gonna come down off this stand and kick your ass.
**Billie Holiday to an audience member
who talked through the show**

Thank you, ladies and gentlemen, for your magnificent indifference.
**Dizzy Gillespie**

You'll have to excuse us. We're progressives. We have to change chords. The only chords that are popular are the ones you can hang yourself with.
**Gerry Mulligan to a Village Vanguard audience**

You sit there in front of me and talk about your crude love affairs...you bare your loosely covered bosoms in front of me and your boyfriends give an embarrassed look up at the bandstand, so you pretend you don't want us to look down into your unveilings.
**Charles Mingus**

Most club owners think you're a traveling vaudeville routine, with a clear-cut act twenty minutes long that's ready to go on four times a night.
**Thelonious Monk**

You, my audience, are all a bunch of poppaloppers. A bunch of tumbling weeds tumbling 'round, running from your subconscious, running from your subconscious unconscious...minds. Minds? Minds that won't let you stop to listen to a word of artistic or meaningful truth.

**Charles Mingus**

HEALTH & AGING:
## Autumn Leaves
*Getting old...there's no future in it, as my father used to say. But the alternatives aren't so hot, either. Jazz musicians take a philosophical look at growing older, staying healthy, and facing mortality.*

If I'd known I was going to live to be a hundred I'd have taken much better care of myself"
**Eubie Blake**

I don't like yogurt, but Dave (Brubeck) is always trying things like that. He's a nutritional masochist. He'll eat anything as long as he figures it's good for him.
**Paul Desmond**

I used to live on wheat germ, peanut butter and bread—I still carry a jar of wheat germ in my instrument case. It's good food.
**Pharoah Sanders**

Not for me. If I want to tune everybody out, I just take off my glasses and enjoy the haze.
**Paul Desmond on contact lenses**

I'm getting too old to play this damn thing and almost too old to carry it.
**Bassist Ray Brown**

You've gotta love livin', baby! Because dyin' is a pain in the ass!
**Frank Sinatra**

People said I'd never make 35, then I'd never make 40, 45; now I'm almost 50, so I'm beginning to think maybe they might be wrong.
**Chet Baker**

I wish I was 90 again
**Eubie Blake**

Maryann, my mother, told me when I was very young. She said "Son, always keep your bowels open, and nothing can harm you."
**Louis Armstrong**

I never heard of a jazz musician who retired. You love what you do, so if you retire, what are you going to do, play for the walls?
**Nat Adderley**

Retire to what?
**Duke Ellington**

Whenever anybody asks me how I keep my hair, I ask them how they keep their teeth. Because I don't have any teeth, you know.
**Jack Teagarden**

If this is good, what the hell did I look like the last time you saw me?
**Brew Moore**

I can't afford to slow down or I can't afford to get old, either. Just have to keep it like it is.
**Wild Bill Davison**

I'm fifty-nine today, but I have the body of a fifty-seven-year-old man.
**Zoot Sims**

Rejoice at the death and cry at the birth: New Orleans sticks close to the scriptures.
**Jelly Roll Morton**

It's the same all over: you fight for your life—until death do you part, and then you got it made.
**Lester Young**

## THE MUSIC BUSINESS: NICE WORK IF YOU CAN GET IT

*Music is sometimes noble and spiritual, but the music business is rotten to the core. Managers who steal from the artists they represent, club owners who only want to fill the club for the lowest possible cost, record companies that don't want to promote the artists they record—these are just a few of the nice folks you'll meet.*

The music business stinks.
**Jaki Byard**

Tastes are *created* by the business interests. How else can you explain the popularity of Al Hirt?
**Charles Mingus**

When you first make a record, you always think, "This is the best thing I've done." And that lasts for anywhere from three to six months, and then you begin to get into the next project and IT becomes your big focus.
**Gary Burton**

If you want to make a living at music, you've got to sell it.
**Dizzy Gillespie**

Always be smarter than the people who hire you.
**Lena Horne**

I ruined a perfectly good hobby by making it my profession.
**Orrin Keepnews on starting his Riverside Records label**

When I was young and very green, I wrote that tune, *Sister Kate*, and someone said that's fine, let me publish it for you. I'll give you fifty dollars. I didn't know nothing about papers and business, and I sold it outright.
**Louis Armstrong**

I'm not selling music, I'm selling excitement.
**Norman Granz on his Jazz at the Philharmonic concerts**

Today everything is done by committee. I mean, nine guys have to get together before they can even put out a record.
**record producer Bob Thiele**

I was really running a music school back then, because my band wasn't making any money. I keep talking about money, because most people don't understand the part of money in running a band.
**Artie Shaw**

The businessmen want jazz to stay just like it is. They can't have Kenny G saying tomorrow, 'I am going to go to Africa and find some pygmies and we're gonna smoke some shit and record and that is my new record!' That used to happen in the '70's, but not now.
**Stanley Clarke**

I just got mad because I didn't have a record contract.
**Marian McPartland on why she started her own record label**

I had gotten a lot of calls from different companies: "Oh, yeah, Chuck, you started that 'smooth jazz' sound and we'd love to have you. Here's what we'd like to do: We'd like the tempo to be like this and it's got to have this sound, and a juggler and three elephants, and...". I was not excited about that.
**Chuck Mangione**

Everything except the music was incredibly bad.  Management, economics, administration, organization...incredibly bad.
**John McLaughlin on his stint with Tony Williams' band Lifetime**

Miles would leave it up to me to make all the fucking decisions.  People today, they want to be producer, writer, they want to do everything.  I'm saying, Jesus Christ, then do it yourself.  Save yourself some money.
**producer Teo Macero**

Those rich millionaires—the Folds and those people—will go over to Paris and buy a Cezanne  or a Goya, pay fifty thousand dollars for it, and put it in a museum.  But we've got our own cultural heritage here and we ignore it.
**Danny Barker**

The *sine quo non* elements in any jazz festival are coherence, artistic honesty, authenticity, and an awareness of when to get through.  After 24 years of jazz festivals I have yet to see one that completely achieved these objectives.
**Leonard Feather**

There is hardly any money interest in art, and music will be there when money is gone.
**Duke Ellington**

I'm so bloody sick of art; I just want to be an entertainer.
**Carla Bley**

You know, most artists think they're above show business, but an artist is not a different person; he just has a different title. The fact that you're an artist doesn't mean that you're not supposed to learn to read and write and count.
**Ornette Coleman**

...There is no doubt that jazz can sell. Will it sell like Michael Jackson? No! There are maybe one or two things on the planet...like velcro, that sell like Michael Jackson.
**T.S. Monk**

If you are a jewelry maker, a watchmaker, and you enjoy a certain kind of handicraft, I don't think it matters that someone later puts the label of Bulova or Wittnauer on the product you have created. That's all after the fact.
**Al Jarreau**

Business is business, jazz is art, and seldom the twain can meet.
**Leonard Feather**

If music lovers knew the wealth of talent being wasted in the name of jazz they'd storm the managers' and bookers' offices and tell them they refuse to settle for the crap they're getting!
**Charles Mingus**

Don't tell me you want to put jazz music out there because you love it so much. Tell me you want to put it out there because you want to sell it. Exploit me a little bit!
**T.S. Monk**

## SWINGING:
## IT DON'T MEAN A THING (IF IT AIN'T GOT THAT SWING)
*Almost all musicians agree that jazz has to swing. But what does it mean to swing? Ah...there's the rub!*

Some stances are just conducive to swinging. If I stand up straight for too long it's harder to swing. Plus my feet hurt.
**Wynton Marsalis**

Things can swing in a lot of different ways. To me, as swing is, swing goes.
**James Moody**

I don't dig that two-beat jive the New Orleans cats play. My boys and I got to have four heavy beats to a bar and no cheating.
**Count Basie**

It's like an act of murder; you play with intent to commit something.
**Duke Ellington**

We all do 'do, re, mi,' but you have got to find the other notes yourself.
**Louis Armstrong**

If the rhythm section isn't swinging, you can forget about it.
**Freddie Green**

I just think swing is a matter of some good things put together that you can really pat your foot by. I can't define it beyond that.
**Count Basie**

If you can't swing you can't swing—You can stuff your stomach with black-eyed peas and chitlins, go out and roll in the mud and say I'm gonna get down, but it ain't going to help if you don't pat your feet right because chitlins have no more to do with soul than mud has to do with music.
**Hampton Hawes**

Intellectualism:
## Brilliant Corners
*Jazz has had more than its share of intellectual artists, fans, writers, and others. Sometimes, though, all that thinking gets in the way of really swinging. A look at the deep thoughts and thinkers.*

It bugs me when people try to analyze jazz as an intellectual theorem. It's not.
**Bill Evans**

This is positively *not* an album to play while you do a doctorate thesis on "Bergson, Webern and Charles the Vicious; Paradox or Ambiguity?"
**Bob Brookmeyer**

Everybody wants to put people on, I think. And get away with it! That's the thing about it: put people on and *get away with it*. That's a science in itself.

**Dizzy Gillespie**

Some of the people who do the most talking about jazz (that may even be the problem right there!) don't seem to get any real fun out of listening to it.

**Gerry Mulligan**

Not to deny that it is a thinking people's music, but when I listen to music if I ever catch myself thinking, I'm in trouble—I know something is wrong.

**Brian Blade**

I've been more used to being written about than being on the writing end. Give me a piano to beat up and that's me; but as to this writing business, I'm like a bear from the fair, I ain't nowhere.

**Fats Waller**

Sometimes I get the feeling that there are orgies going on all over New York City, and somebody says, 'Let's call Desmond,' and somebody else says, 'Why bother? He's probably home reading the Encyclopedia Britannica.'

**Paul Desmond**

You know, I've been following the Kenton band for years, and the only things I ever liked were "Peanut Vendor,""Lover", "How High the Moon", and things like that. It's a shame; this could have been a real swinging band, but it failed because Stan read a few books or something.

**Norman Granz**

West Coast jazz is just the sound of guys who played on the West Coast, if it means anything.

**Dave Brubeck**

I think I might take a second to delve into the cosmological and metaphysical aspects of this composition. I think we can say quite simply that the transcendental character of the composition is based on two very definitely Freudian concepts...The whole relationship between this concept and certain basic concepts of, say, James Joyce, is the fact that motorcycle riders find salted popcorn extremely good under those conditions.
**Stan Kenton Arranger Bill Russo**

## ECCENTRICITY:
### TWISTED
*Jazz musicians are probably no more eccentric than the average Joe, it's just that their behavior tends to be examined under a microscope, and often their difficult behavior is admired and imitated by others. Sometimes, too, they act crazier than they actually are...*

Anybody who goes to a psychiatrist ought to have his head examined.
**Dave Lambert**

Bud was always ... a little on the borderline.
**Dexter Gordon on Bud Powell**

You think he is crazy? I taught him to act that way.
**Charlie Parker, referring to Bud Powell**

Sometimes it's to your advantage for people to think you're crazy.
**Thelonious Monk**

Say that I'm uncooperative, and that I don't want to be in the book. I'm not a jazz musician anyway.
**Charles Mingus**

Never talk to anybody on the telephone unless you're lying flat on your back in the bed.
**Duke Ellington**

The outer space beings are my brothers. They sent me here. They already know my music.
**Sun Ra**

Yeah, Stan's a nice bunch of guys.
**Zoot Sims on Stan Getz**

Improvisation is the ability to talk to one's self.
**Cecil Taylor**

Jazz is neurotic.
**Stan Kenton**

If you think this is weird, just take a look at yourselves.
**Charles Mingus to an unappreciative audience**

Thelonious Monk.... was not exactly "the boy next door".
**Dexter Gordon**

If someone has been escaping reality, I don't expect him to dig my music.
**Charles Mingus**

Thelonious Monk went over to Bird and to Bud (Powell) and said, "I told you guys to act crazy, but I didn't tell you to fall in love with the act. You're really crazy now".
**Charles Mingus**

People always thought I was crazy, so I used that to my own advantage to attract public attention and find the most universal audience for our music.
**Dizzy Gillespie**

Yeah, Dizzy's crazy—crazy like a fox.
**Unknown**

Man, that cat is nuts!
**Thelonious Monk on Ornette Coleman**

I don't know if you've ever seen Monk perform, but Monk would dance up onstage. Monk would start dancing and a lot of these straight-laced jazz critics would be there and they didn't know what to say: "Wait a minute, this is such profound, deep music – and there he is dancing!" They couldn't reconcile the two things.
**Sonny Rollins**

In my private life I am seldom eccentric. I do order fifteen suits of clothes at a time and then stick to one of them.
**Duke Ellington**

Perhaps it is a peculiarity of mine that despite the fact that I am a professional performer, it is true that I have always preferred playing without an audience
**Bill Evans**

I'm sick and tired of those sugary jazzmen, those effeminate players with their watered-down sounds. And do you know what's causing it? Mothers. More and more they're dominating their sons so that virility is missing in so many young men.
**Stan Kenton**

What's interesting about a person without problems?
**Carla Bley**

## WOMEN IN JAZZ:
## Have You Met Miss Jones
*Women have been playing jazz pretty much as long as it has existed, but they have generally been a distinct minority. Here are some thoughts about women playing jazz and some thoughts from the women themselves.*

Jazz is a male language. It's a matter of speaking that language and women just can't do it.
**Anonymous male pianist**

One more girl band is about all this country needs to send it right back into the depths of the Depression.
*Saturday Evening Post,* **1936**

Why is it that outside of a few sepia females the woman musician was never born, capable of "sending" anyone farther than the nearest exit?
*Downbeat* Magazine, **1938**

Only God can make a tree...and only men can play good jazz.
**George T. Simon**

I wonder if it would surprise the women instrumentalists of the 1930s and '40s to hear that some fifty and sixty years after their days as young players facing stereotypes and ignorance, I still hear that I'm the first woman saxophonist that someone has ever seen.
**Leigh Pilzer**

After thirty-five years, I *am* tired of wearing gowns on the bandstand.
**Carline Ray**

People talk about how art reflects life, but if jazz is art, how can it reflect life if there are only men playing it?
**Susie Ibarra**

They don't think of you as a woman if you can really play.
**Mary Lou Williams**

A lot of women think—they look at themselves, they look at men, they say "You're a woman. You write music. Therefore, I'm a woman, *I* can write music." The one doesn't follow the other at all, any more than that all redheads are astronauts.
**Carla Bley**

If Gene Krupa were a woman, how long do you suppose he would be an ace drummer in Benny Goodman's band? In evening gown, he might still be sensational even hampered by brassiere straps, girdle, skirt, and high heels—but Mrs. G.K. or Miss Anybody couldn't make a one night stand with bags under her eyes.

**Peggy Gilbert**

## Race:
## (What Did I Do To Be So) Black And Blue

*Race is a delicate issue in America, and jazz music steps squarely in the middle of it. You can't really look at the music or its history without confronting America's legacy of racial prejudice and inequality. Musicians, black and white, have dealt with the issue in many different ways, as these remarks make clear.*

For all the people who don't know what segregation is, they should try to find a few history books to find out what it was all about so they'd know how to treat certain people.

**Marshall Royal**

Personally, I think everyone can see that I'm black, so I guess I don't have to tell anybody about it.

**Ray Charles**

When I was a kid, some of the guys would try to get me to hate white people for what they've been doing to Negroes, and for a while I tried real hard. But every time I got to hating them, some white guy would come along and mess the whole thing up.

**Thelonious Monk**

The Afro-American experience is the only real culture that America has. Basically, every American tries to walk, talk, dress and behave like African Americans.

**Hugh Masakela**

Blacks thought I was talking about whites. But I was talking about everybody.

**Sun Ra**

I should like to be alive in 500 years when we'll all be one race, all be mixed. I hate the racial thing.
**Stan Getz**

One thing you can be sure of, though. As long as I'm in America, I'll never in my life work with a white band again.
**Roy Eldridge**

Occasionally an interviewer would ask 'Do you feel as though coming to Africa is coming home?' And I'm just not set up to lie. My answer was, 'No, my home is in Las Vegas.'
**Joe Williams**

I got a simple rule about everybody. If you don't treat me right — shame on you!
**Louis Armstrong**

You know somethin', man? Some day I'm gonna be walking' up the street one way and you gonna be comin' down the other way, and we gonna pass each other and I'm gonna say "Hello, best white band in the world", and you gonna say, "Hello, best colored band in the world."
**Chick Webb to Artie Shaw**

One night we were playing in Atlanta, Georgia, and this guy hollered at me "Hey there, boy, how come you got a white girl up there on the piano?" I just looked him straight in the eye and said, "Sorry sir, I thought I just had a pianist."
**Art Blakey**

Yeah, there are certain things in this life that nobody likes to talk about. Nobody white, that is.
**Charles Mingus**

I'll be playing a maid, but she's really a cute maid.
**Billie Holiday on her film debut in *New Orleans***

You're the right color but you're still a stupid motherfucker.
**Miles Davis to a black record producer**

Anybody that knows his horns don't pay much attention to color.
**Louis Armstrong**

They would even beat Jesus if He was black and marched.
**Louis Armstrong on racial violence in Selma, Alabama, 1965**

This whole racial thing is a lot of shit, from all the way down all the way to the top. And the closer you get to the top, the more it disappears.
**Art Farmer**

My theory is that a note doesn't give a fuck who plays it, as long as he plays it well.
**Clark Terry**

No white man ever contributed anything to the development of jazz.
**French critic Andre Hodeir**

## Politics, History, & Culture:
## Oh Lord Don't Let Them Drop That Atomic Bomb On Me
*Jazz cats do not shy away from political and cultural topics, as you'll definitely see in this section.*

History bores the shit out of me.
**Joe Zawinul**

I say give the musicians a shot! They can't make the planet any worse...I don't know though, let me stop and think about this. I wouldn't want some of the musicians I've known to be in charge. No, take the creative people out!
**Anthony Braxton**

Culture is like wine. You have *chardonnay, merlot, pinot noir*. People don't say, 'Let's water it down so the kids can have some, too.' Music is culture.
**Lenny White**

The further jazz moves away from the stark blue continuum and the collective realities of Afro-American and American life, the more it moves into academic concert-hall lifelessness, which can be replicated by any middle class showing off its music lessons.

**Amiri Baraka (Leroi Jones)**

What's in a name? Nothing! Cats say, "Call me Muhammed so-and-so." But what's the difference?

**Art Blakey**

I wasn't the type of guy to go steal your horn and pawn it. If I were going to do illegal activities, I was going to beat the banks, the government, and the insurance companies. Those were the biggest thieves anyway in American life, and they were legal thieves.

**Red Rodney**

When Ronald Reagan was elected I was on a bus traveling with a band in France. I got a piece of paper and wrote a little arrangement of *The Star Spangled Banner* in a minor key. That was how we opened the show that night in Paris.

**Carla Bley**

After tonight I'd vote for him if he were running for Grand Dragon of the Ku Klux Klan.

**Comment on Richard Nixon by a musician at the celebration of Duke Ellington's 70th birthday at the White House**

Oscar Peterson is so well informed and well organized that I'm sure, if he wanted to, he could run for office in Toronto.

**Norman Granz**

# Quotable Jazz

I'm a radical for personal freedom and liberty. I'm disappointed in Nixon. He came in on one set of principles, then operated on another. Why, if a left-winger had made some of those same proposals, everybody would be up in arms!
**Don Ellis**

More and more I am finding myself bugged, or at least uninterested in, the whole notion of nationalistic pride attached to successful music—any music.
**Pat Metheny**

This is America – we still have the opportunity to find out things. The libraries are still open. There are still books being produced. Nobody's banning books or burning books. We can find out things ourselves.
**Sonny Rollins**

...If I'm playing Klezmer stuff, people can think that I'm all these different kinds of people that I'm not. They can think I'm down with killing Palestinians, but I'm not. They can think that, you know, because that's the person that they project me to be.
**Don Byron**

Normal moral repressions may vanish. A fatalistic spending spree will appear. Flesh and blood entertainment will be most appealing. Money and jobs will be more plentiful. It will be our job to keep emotions normal and healthy.
***Downbeat* Magazine on the effects of WWII on society and the role jazz musicians could play**

I fluffed off the guy who kept requesting tunes all night, then found out he was the King's son.
**Duke Ellington on meeting George, Duke of Kent**

If America wouldn't honor its constitution and respect us as men, we couldn't give a shit about the American way.
**Kenny Clarke**

I would like to kill him. I think that's the best thing that I could do in my life. Kill him. To talk to him is impossible. He's kind of this tough guy, and what you're going to hear is a mono-logue from him. You're going to listen to him talking to you. But it's not going to be a conversation.
**Arturo Sandoval on Fidel Castro**

I have a theory, man. Bad things in this world come from the south. Look at the South of our country. South Vietnam. South Africa. Stalin was born in the south of Russia...I figure I'll stay as far north as possible.
**George Russell**

I am prior to borders.
**Antonio Carlos Jobim**

## Religion, Spirituality and Philosophy:
### Better Git It In Your Soul
*Even though jazz has historically been thought of as "the Devil's music", it comes from a tradition rich in spirituality. Of course, as with everything else, musicians interpret the spiritual a little differently than some folks.*

I am a devout musician.
**Charlie Parker**

I'm a Baptist and a good friend of the Pope's and I always wear a Jewish star a friend gave me for luck.
**Louis Armstrong when asked if he is a religious man**

Actually, I'm not interested in Zen that much, as a philoso-phy, nor in joining any movements. I don't pretend to under-stand it. I just find it comforting.
**Bill Evans**

When people ask me how it is that I was a musician I face-tiously say that I'm a firm believer in reincarnation and in a previous life I was Johann Sebastian Bach's guide dog.
**George Shearing**

## Quotable Jazz

The trumpeter Roy Eldridge once told a guy he could only reach a divine state in performance 4 or 5 times a year. That sounds about right for me.

**Sonny Rollins**

I must be from some place else in the universe, because I'm a total misfit. I can't get with none of this.

**Johnny Griffin**

As far as I'm concerned, Hippocrates was the first hippy, a guy who was smug because he thought he knew something. Socrates was wise because he realized how little he knew.

**Bill Evans**

I'm very glad to have met you. I like your playing very much.

**Charlie Parker to Jean-Paul Sartre**

I wanted to become a rabbi. I got as far as becoming a cantor.

**Willie "The Lion" Smith**

## RECORDS & RECORDING:
## Nights at the Turntable

*A few comments on the recording industry and records.*

There was once a joke that in the year 2045 someone brought out a *Best of Keith Jarrett* set in the currently fashionable laser-hologram/virtual reality format. It consisted of 87 LHVR diskettes. (There was an audiophile vinyl option, but you needed your own truck to take it home.)

**Richard Cook and Brian Morton**

Back in the '50s high fidelity was the big thing, but I considered it something of a con by the record companies, especially when they began putting 'high fidelity' stickers on LPs that had been in their catalogues for years.
**Norman Granz**

Sometimes I suspect that the universe is on tape and that someday someone will be able to play back any sound ever made.
**Mose Allison**

The difference between *Blue Note* and every other jazz label is two days' rehearsal.
**Anonymous**

## Fame:
## I Should Care

*Sometimes musicians seem bitter about being passed over for fame, other times they seem to avoid it like the plague.*

I'm famous. Ain't that a bitch!
**Thelonious Monk**

Fate is being kind to me. Fate doesn't want me to be too famous too young.
**Duke Ellington**

I, certainly, will never become a success, so I don't have to worry about it.
**Cecil Taylor**

History avenges itself, and this is history, the history of music. Whether I get the recognition now, it will all come out. Because the records are out and the records are...well, a matter of record.
**Dizzy Gillespie**

I'm a new star, according to a magazine in England, and I don't even have fare to England.
**Albert Ayler**

Tote that Down Beat, win that poll, hope I get a mention before I'm too old!
**Charles Mingus**

I'm not worried about creating music for posterity, I just want it to sound good right now!
**Duke Ellington**

## MISTAKES:
## Everything Happens to Me

*Everyone hits a wrong note or plays a wrong chord change. Some thoughts on making the best of a bad situation.*

If you're gonna make a mistake, make it so loud everybody else sounds wrong.
**Joe Venuti**

Yes, those wrong notes are intentional.
**Ben Allison**

If you hit a wrong note, then make it right by what you play afterwards.
**Joe Pass**

I've built a whole career out of making mistakes!
**Lester Bowie**

Tonight we got to make history. Our future depends on tonight. So I don't want any excuses. I don't want nobody drunk, I don't want nobody to miss; anybody do any little thing wrong, don't look for me to give you notice. Just pack and go home because this is my life!
**Chick Webb on the eve of his battle with Benny Goodman's band at the Savoy Ballroom**

### GANGSTERS:
## Heavy Weather

*Since jazz music was often played around alcohol, prostitution, and gambling in its early days, it was inevitable that musicians should come up against the gangsters at some point.*

You know gangsters run jazz.
**Charles Mingus**

If there are gangsters, they aren't interested in Mingus. If they were, he wouldn't be out of work, he'd be dead in an alley someplace.
**Billy Taylor**

If it wasn't for pimps, prostitutes, hustlers, gangsters, and gamblers there wouldn't be no jazz! They supported the club owners who bought the music. It wasn't the middle-class people who said "Let's go hear Charlie Parker tonight."
**Betty Carter**

If it had been left to the so-called decent people in this country there'd be no jazz. It was due to the Mafia, who liked the music and ran the joints—Sicily you know is only 28 miles from Africa, so they have a great affinity.
**Jon Hendricks**

Once or twice I saw a killing in a club...Like a gangster come in one night before a show and started shooting the lights out...But I never knew any musician that ever got hurt or in trouble, if he just kept his mouth shut and tended to his own business.
**Wild Bill Davison**

One night a bunch of tough guys came in and started turning tables over to introduce themselves...To us they said "You boys keep playing if you don't want to get hurt". That's all. And you know who kept playing.
**Jimmy McPartland**

## LIFE LESSONS:
## In a Mellotone

*Some thoughts to help you on your journey through this life, whether as a musician or just a regular cat. Taking these comments to heart will definitely help you to live a good, clean, satisfying life. I think.*

The bad jazz that a cat blows wails long after he's cut out; the groovy is often stashed with their frames.
**Lord Buckley paraphrasing *Julius Caesar***

A true gentleman is a man who knows how to play the accordion and doesn't.
**George Shearing**

I discovered early in life that if you take gym first period, you can go into the wrestling room and sit in the corner and sleep.
**Paul Desmond**

When the chord changes, you should change.
**Joe Pass**

I don't let my mouth say nothin' my head can't stand.
**Louis Armstrong**

Not too slow, not too fast. Kind of half-fast.
**Louis Armstrong**

You cannot get a degree in physics if you don't know something about algebra.
**Marcus Roberts**

The hippest thing you can do is not play at all. Just listen.
**Lennie Tristano**

As long as you've got your horn in your mouth, you're developing.
**Zoot Sims**

Either your instrument handles you or you handle the instrument. You're not tripping through tulips with it.
**Eddie "Lockjaw" Davis**

Only play what you hear. If you don't hear anything, don't play anything.
**Chick Corea**

When they play fast, you play slow. When they play slow, you play fast.
**Miles Davis to Buster Williams**

You know, they put all kinds of stuff in toothpaste, but you don't go out and find what it is. They might put anything in toothpaste. You don't worry about what they got in it. You use it, and that's it.
**Ornette Coleman**

If you take care of the music, the music will take care of you.
**Dewey Redman**

We probably do most of our listening in the car. As a matter of fact, my last car ride I listened to side one of *Frampton Comes Alive* so it shows you where I'm at.
**John Pizzarelli**

When people say 'The new pop songs aren't as good as the old pop songs,' I say, 'Listen again.' It's just ridiculous to think that good songwriting ended in the '50s. We're in 2002, and you're telling me no one has written a good melody and good lyrics in 50 years?
**Cassandra Wilson**

No matter how carefully and assiduously and how deeply you bury shit, the American public will find it and buy it in large quantity. It's true, absolutely true.

**Artie Shaw**

## III. MUSICIANS SPEAKING FREELY

### MUSICIANS ON MUSICIANS:
### Something to Remember You By

Brubeck, for instance, is not careless. He's a studied guy. And even if his picture ends up on the back cover of *Life,* he's still a studious guy.

**Eddie Condon**

When he's most interesting, he sounds like me.

**Cecil Taylor on Dave Brubeck**

Paul Desmond sounds like a female alcoholic.

**Eddie Condon**

Let's face it—we'd all sound like that if we could.

**John Coltrane on Stan Getz**

He only plays piano when he's bugged.

**Art Farmer on Gerry Mulligan**

Some little people has music in them, but Fats, he was *all* music, and you know how big he was.

**James P. Johnson**

First you speak of Art Tatum, then take a long deep breath, and you speak of the other pianists.

**Dizzy Gillespie**

Finally Beiderbecke took out a silver cornet. He put it to his lips and blew a phrase. The sound came out like a girl saying 'yes.' "
**Eddie Condon on Bix Beiderbecke**

Bix's breaks were not as wild as Armstrong's, but they were hot and he selected each note with musical care. His music affected me in a different way. Can't tell you how-like licorice, you have to eat some.
**Hoagy Carmichael on Bix Beiderbecke**

First of all, I swore it was two people playing. When I finally admitted to myself that was one man, I gave up the piano for a month. I figured it was hopeless to practice.
**Oscar Peterson on hearing Art Tatum for the first time**

The first time I heard an Oscar Peterson record, I said to myself, 'There, that's a white who has worked hard at the piano and thinks he sounds black.'
**Jimmy Smith**

Listening to Herschel and Lester was like watching a tennis match. You just dug them both-and it wasn't a question of one cutting the other. It was like what do you want for breakfast, ham and eggs or bacon and eggs?
**Jo Jones on the Count Basie band featuring saxophonists Herschel Evans and Lester Young**

I fell asleep the last time I heard the Modern Jazz Quartet in person.
**Kenny Clarke**

FAMOUS MEETINGS:
## I Want to Talk About You
When I first met him I said: "Mr. Tatum, I've been listening to your records for years, and I've copied so many of your things. I'm really overjoyed to meet you." And he said: "Glad to meet you, son. Gonna buy me a beer?"
**George Shearing on meeting Art Tatum**

You could be my son. You even look like me a little bit...Say, who's your mother?
**Fats Waller to Bobby Short**

Look, you come in here tomorrow, and anything you do with your right hand I'll do with my left.
**Art Tatum to Bud Powell**

Don't give a damn what key we playing in, you ain't going to play. So you just might as well get on down off the stage.
**Count Basie to Art Tatum**

## INFLUENCES:
## I've Got You Under My Skin

I am my own influences. Other people don't influence me, I influence *them*.
**Ahmad Jamal**

I got a lot of licks to steal yet. I'm not through stealing.
**Phil Woods**

I stole everything that I heard, but mostly I stole from the horns.
**Ella Fitzgerald**

Even though I'd listened to Sonny Rollins, it still didn't prepare me for Coleman Hawkins. His sense of time, it had a certain severity and I wasn't ready for it. It was like giving somebody a 1945 Chateau Lafitte and they've never had wine before.
**Lew Tabackin**

Most of the soloists at Birdland had to wait for Parker's next record in order to find out what to play next. What will they do now?
**Charles Mingus**

Paul Desmond's big contribution is going to be that he didn't copy Charlie Parker.
**Dave Brubeck**

I prefer that nobody teach me. I prefer to swing on my own.
**Stephane Grappelli**

I used to have old cats tell me, "You're going to be a great player in time." A young guy don't want to hear that crap, but you know they're right.
**Nick Brignola**

When I first came down to the United States from Canada, I came with stars in my eyes. When you hear great artists, as I did on records, you inevitably build up a certain amount of personal respect for them. But when you see some of them, it's apt to be another thing altogether.
**Oscar Peterson**

I think we've all had enough of Coltrane saxophonists. *There's* a case of somebody ruining a generation of saxophonists, as Louis Armstrong may have ruined a generation or two of trumpet players.
**Paul Bley**

I tell people: I was a high school dropout, but I graduated from Art Blakey College, the Miles Davis Conservatory of Music, and Charlie Parker University.
**Walter Bishop Jr.**

## Ego:
## I'm Nothin' Without Me

Interviewer: Why do you think you won the (*Downbeat* readers') poll?

Dexter Gordon: Because I'm the world's greatest tenor saxophonist, ha, ha, ha! No, I really don't know.
**Downbeat** Magazine

I played for Billy Eckstine. But I said "What am I doing?" After I got through playing about ten or twelve numbers, then he'd say, "And incidentally, people, how about a nice hand for..." This is not my role.
**Tadd Dameron**

It is evidently known, beyond contradiction, that New Orleans is the cradle of jazz, and I, myself, happened to be creator in the year 1902, many years before the Dixieland Band organized.
**Jelly Roll Morton**

I don't care what you think of my saxophone playing. I'm still the greatest fisherman in the world.
**Flip Phillips**

I first met Jelly Roll in Chicago. He was livin' high then. You know, Jelly was a travelin' cat, sharp and good lookin' and always bragging about he wrote this and that and the other thing—in fact, everything! And let me tell you this—no one ever won an argument with Jelly either!
**Zutty Singleton**

I always called him the Dizzy Dean of music, he was so belligerent and braggadocio...But, one thing I always noticed about Jelly, he would back up everything he *said* by what he could *do*.
**Omer Simeon on Jelly Roll Morton**

That's me: jack-of-all-trades, master of one.
**John Scofield**

If they come to hear me play, it's not like coming to hear Bill Evans play. They have to work at it. I don't expect people who listen to Emerson, Lake, and Palmer to come hear me. I accept that reality.
**Cecil Taylor**

Everything I do is Mingus.
**Charles Mingus**

My music has to get past me, and I'm too vain to play anything I think is bad.
**Miles Davis**

Mr. Zawinul, I was at the concert. It was OK. By the way, let me introduce myself. My name is John Francis Pastorious III, I'm the greatest bass player in the world.
**Jaco Pastorious, quoted by Joe Zawinul**

Kansas City style, Chicago style, New Orleans style hell, they're all Jelly Roll style.
**Jelly Roll Morton**

## Self-Criticism:
## Here's That Rainy Day

The trouble is, I'm like an architect who designs a house but doesn't want to spend time figuring out where to put the couch or what color curtains to have. I just get sort of bored when it comes to the interior decoration of a piece.
**Carla Bley**

I simply want to reach a level where I will never cease to make progress. . . . So that, even on the bad evenings, I may never be bad enough to despair.
**Sonny Rollins**

I'm a very sad tuba player. My very first recording in 1930 was with Tiny Porham and I'm playing tuba on this record. If you want to know why I'm playing bass now, just listen to this record.
**Milt Hinton**

I can't say I ever actually switched to bass—it was just that there was always a need for a bass player, and I was a rotten trumpet player.
**Steve Swallow**

I have won several prizes as the world's slowest alto player, as well as a special award in 1961 for quietness.
**Paul Desmond**

It's taken me all my life to learn what not to play.
**Dizzy Gillespie**

I don't like lightweight stuff, even the stuff I did with Miles, I didn't like so much. Too light!
**Joe Zawinul**

I have never made a solo that I would recommend anybody to hear. No, I've never been satisfied with any solo I've ever played, I always thought I could do better.
**Harry "Sweets" Edison**

I am the world's laziest writer.
**Oscar Peterson**

### Insults & Feuds:
## I'll Be Glad When You're Dead, You Rascal You

He was a pain in the neck
**Bernie Privin on Tommy Dorsey**

Get up from that piano. You hurtin' its feelings.
**Jelly Roll Morton**

I've never heard anything Wynton played sound like it meant anything at all. Wynton has no voice and no presence. His music sounds like a talented high-school trumpet player to me...He's jazzy the same way someone who drives a BMW is sporty
**Keith Jarrett on Wynton Marsalis**

It seems like the older he gets, the more *regular* his playing becomes.
**Wynton Marsalis on Keith Jarrett**

I love Keith (Jarrett), but I'm mad at him because he always turns me down for *Piano Jazz*.
**Marian McPartland**

He sounded to me like he's supposed to be the savior of jazz. Sometimes people speak as though someone asked them a question. Well, nobody asked him a question.
**Miles Davis on Wynton Marsalis**

He's got a lot of technique, but that's about it.
**Miles Davis on Wynton Marsalis**

Man, get the fuck off the stage.
**Miles Davis to Wynton Marsalis at the 1986
Vancouver Jazz Festival**

Here's this cat, obviously, obviously—everybody *knows* this cat ain't got it. But they keep on pressing: 'He's got the technique and any day he's gonna come up with this astounding new development.' Believe me, it ain't gonna happen...Wynton is a good musician, but he's been totally miscast. No way in the world is he the king of jazz, the king of trumpet...
**Lester Bowie on Wynton Marsalis**

The Lord didn't stop giving out talent with Duke Ellington...Wynton thinks he's the end. But why do we only have to play Duke? You've got to bring something to the table.
**Betty Carter**

In 1908 Handy didn't know anything about the blues and he doesn't know anything about jazz and stomps to this day . . . I myself figured out the peculiar form of mathematics and harmonies that was strange to all the world but me.
**Jelly Roll Morton, Disputing that W. C. Handy was the "Father of the Blues; in "I Discovered Blues in 1902," in *Downbeat* Magazine**

Now that we've been put through the socioeconomic racial forensics of a jazz-illiterate historian and a self-imposed jazz expert prone to sophomoric generalizations and ultraconservative politically correct (for now) utterances...can we have some films about jazz by people who actually understand the music itself?
**Keith Jarrett on *Ken Burns' Jazz***

Music isn't baseball; there are no statistics for measuring achievement, and Burns is as entitled to his opinions as I am to mine — even if his seem to come wholesale from Marsalis and company.
**Francis Davis on *Ken Burns' Jazz***

There is a chapter in (my) book on Fusion, which is there precisely because you can't leave it out of the story. You can if you're Ken Burns, but you can't if you're really going to take a serious view of what's happened to that whole movement.
**Alyn Shipton**

I don't mind being the butt of a joke—if it's a funny joke.
**Kenny G.**

When the torch got passed to Wynton the historian, and he took control, that's when jazz actually died. He put down Kenny

G., but the truth is Kenny G. was playing himself. Kenny G. is a fake white boy. *Great!* That's who Kenny is. The question is, "Wynton Marsalis, who are you?"
**Leon Parker**

But when Kenny G decided that it was appropriate for him to defile the music of the man who is probably the greatest jazz musician that has ever lived by spewing his lame-ass, jive, pseudo bluesy, out-of-tune, noodling, wimped out, fucked up playing all over one of the great Louis' tracks (even one of his lesser ones), he did something that I would not have imagined possible. He...shit all over the graves of all the musicians past and present who have risked their lives by going out there on the road for years and years developing their own music inspired by the standards of grace that Louis Armstrong brought to every single note he played over an amazing lifetime as a musician.
**Pat Metheny on Kenny G's overdubbed "duet" with Louis Armstrong on "What a Wonderful World"**

If I ever DO see him anywhere, at any function - he WILL get a piece of my mind and maybe a guitar wrapped around his head.
**Pat Metheny on Kenny G.**

I think he was the most tacky guy in the world. It was something I had to do. I was desperate, what can I say?
**Bebel Gilberto on recording "The Girl From Ipanema"with Kenny G**

He did show a knack for connecting to the basest impulses of the large crowd by deploying his two or three most effective licks (holding long notes and playing fast runs—never mind that there were lots of harmonic clams in them) at the key moments to elicit a powerful crowd reaction (over and over again). The other main thing I noticed was that he also, as he does to this day, played horribly out of tune—consistently sharp.
**Pat Metheny on Kenny G**

### Lawrence Welk:
## Grandpa's Spells
*What the hell is Lawrence Welk doing in a book of jazz quotations? Well, his name just kept coming up...*

And now, Ladies and Gentlemen, we're going to play that old Duke Ellington standard: 'Take a Train.'
**Lawrence Welk**

Lawrence Welk kept me sober, and it damn near killed me. He was pretty hard on drinking.
**Pete Fountain**

A lot of people resented any comment on their records from a musician. They'd rather have had Lawrence Welk or Adolf Hitler or someone say something about their records—as long as he said something good.
**Trumpeter Ruby Braff on his stint as a record reviewer**

Lawrence Welk came to hear us when we were in Tucson the other night. He seemed to enjoy it, and he sure got his sinuses cleared, because he was at the front table.
**Woody Herman**

## IV. STYLES, PEOPLE, and PLACES

### Big Bands & Swing:
## Stompin' At the Savoy

Swing? Well, that's what they're calling it this year.
**Duke Ellington, 1938**

It was swing and sweat with Charlie Barnet like it was swing and sway with Sammy Kaye.
**Dick Meldonian**

Traveling with a big band is like being an inmate in a traveling zoo.
**Hoagy Carmichael**

Tommy Dorsey was the last of the band leaders...He was always ahead of his time, if he got drunk he was difficult, but then who the hell isn't difficult if you get drunk...
**Dick Haymes**

Somebody asked me once, "Do you think that swing will ever come back?" And I said, "Do you think the 1938 Ford will ever come back?"
**Artie Shaw**

I think that band (Glenn Miller) was the beginning of the end. It was a mechanized version of what they called jazz music. I still can't stand to listen to it.
**Artie Shaw**

He had a big band, but he handled it as though it were six pieces.
**Dicky Wells on Count Basie**

Stan Kenton killed the dance-band business.
**Charlie Barnet**

They turn around and they name Paul Whiteman the "King of Swing", you know, and the only way he could swing is from a rope.
**Art Blakey**

If I'd known it was an era, I'd have paid more attention. All I remember is sleeping in the back of the bus.
**Helen O'Connell**

The truth is, you could take all the swing bands on earth and drop them into the middle of the Pacific; and, given civilization just as we knew it before, you'd probably have swing music back, going strong, in less than six months.
**Duke Ellington**

Are big bands coming back? Sure, every football season.
**Woody Herman**

Count Basie was college, but Duke Ellington was graduate school.
**Clark Terry**

I ran a tight ship. No dope, no booze, no hard language—we became known as the milk shake band.
**Les Brown**

Dance music—as I keep saying, you can dance to a windshield wiper...a windshield wiper that's fairly steady gives you a beat and all you need's an out-of-tune tenor playing "Melancholy Baby" and you've got dance music.
**Artie Shaw**

## BEBOP:
## Salt Peanuts

The unhep, then unhip, then corny music magazine *Down Beat* actually had to re-review the bop classics because they had torn their ass so bad when they reviewed the records when they first came out...
**Amiri Baraka (LeRoi Jones)**

There's no such thing as bop music, but there's such a thing as progress.
**Coleman Hawkins**

If a guy is gonna play good bop he has to have a sort of a bop soul.
**Count Basie**

Bebop didn't have the humanity of Duke Ellington. It didn't even have that recognizable thing. Bird and Diz were great, fantastic, challenging—but they weren't sweet.
**Miles Davis**

Bebop has set music back twenty years.
**Tommy Dorsey**

Many of the harmonic structures of bebop come from Stravinsky, from Handel and Bartok, so to say "black music"—I don't know what that is, unless it would be some African drums or something.

**Dexter Gordon**

As long as they say I've got a great band, I don't care if they say it's bop or what.

**Dizzy Gillespie**

Even after 45 years of absorbing bebop I don't believe that Monk's chords are exactly comforting.

**Robert Christigau**

Playing "bop" is like playing Scrabble with all the vowels missing.

**Duke Ellington**

Bop is no love-child of jazz.

**Charlie Parker**

(Charlie) Parker himself, compulsively fast and showy, couldn't play four bars without resorting to a peculiarly irritating five-note cliché from a pre-war song called "The Woody Woodpecker song".

**Philip Larkin**

To me, bebop is a collection of nauseating clichés, repeated *ad infinitum*.

**John Hammond**

Bebop sounds to me like a hardware store in an earthquake.

**Jimmy Cannon**

All I did was sing "How High the Moon". It seemed like the only song I ever sang.
### Ella Fitzgerald on the bebop years

Clinkers pass easily in bop. Since it is doubtful whether a planned melodic line exists in most solos at up-tempo, and since the bizarre is normal, complete fluffs must be greeted by a dubious silence.
### D. Leon Wolff, *Downbeat* Magazine, 1949

You see, pops, that's the kind of talk that's ruining the music. Everybody trying to do something new, no one trying to learn the fundamentals first. All them young cats playing them weird chords. And what happens? No one's working.
### Louis Armstrong

Kansas City, eh? Well, I guess everyone got some kind of bell that gets a tap from that town. It ain't no good this year and hasn't been for some time. I think the boppers killed it, but then I'm prejudiced so we'll leave that lie.
### Bob Brookmeyer

Just look at (52nd Street) today. Don't let me tell you nothing. Just look at the Street. They've thrown out the bands and put in a lot of chicks taking their clothes off. That's what that bop music has done for the business.
### Louis Armstrong

One bebopper walked up to another and said, "Are you gonna flat your fifths tonight?" The other one answered, "No, I'm going to drink mine." That's a typical joke about beboppers.
### Dizzy Gillespie

Bop is at the end of the road. Now everybody wants dance music.
### Dizzy Gillespie

Some guys said "Here's bop!" Wham! They said, "Here's something we can make money on!" Wham! "Here's a comedian" Wham! "Here's a guy who talks funny talk."

**Charlie Parker**

As we walked in, see, these cats snatched up their horns and blew crazy stuff. One would stop all of a sudden and another would start for no reason at all. We never could tell when a solo was supposed to begin or end. Then they all quit at once and walked off the stand. It scared us.

**Dave Tough**

If you got up on the bandstand at Minton's and couldn't play, you were not only going to be embarrassed by people ignoring you or booing you, you might get your ass kicked.

**Miles Davis**

Cab (Calloway) would turn around and say "What the hell you got to play that damn Chinese music for?"

**Milt Hinton**

It's one of those bop records in the sense that I detest it. No stars.

**Sy Oliver (*Downbeat* Magazine blindfold test)**

Bebop is not, never was, and never will be true jazz if it has a beat or not.

**Buck Clayton**

Why do they ignore me? Only because I'm funny. Do I intend to stop being funny? Hell no! If the music goes, I can always go on the stage as a comedian!

**Dizzy Gillespie**

(Bop) has been...called development. But there are different kinds of development; a hot bath can develop into a cold one.

**Philip Larkin**

## FREE JAZZ:
## Freedom Jazz Dance

Look, if you play the wrong chord, it's the wrong chord. It doesn't matter how free you think you are—it's the wrong chord.
**Ruby Braff**

Well, the last refuge of the untalented is the avant-garde.
**George Russell**

Experimental means you're trying to do something. I'm *doing* it.
**Cecil Taylor**

Some people say I can't play the changes, some people say I can't play in tune, and some people say I can't play the saxophone. My basic response is I'm doing the best I can.
**John Zorn**

Tenor-men Sonny Rollins, John Coltrane, John Griffin, and Ornette Coleman will compete in a "bad note" contest. The one who plays two choruses in a row without hitting a clinker wins a special award from *Metronome* magazine.
**Tom Scanlon**

We are not angry men. We are outraged.
**Archie Shepp**

The only semblance of collectivity lies in the fact that these eight nihilists were collected together in one studio at one time with one common cause: to destroy the music that gave them birth. Give them top marks for the attempt.
**John Tynan on Ornette Coleman's album *Free Jazz***

When you come to New York, there's a whole school of musicians who are called the avant-garde, and you don't really need any craft requirements to join their ranks. All you have to do is be black and have an African name...
**Wynton Marsalis**

There are a whole bunch of cats who can't run the changes but they play a lot of that far out stuff. When you ask them 'What was that?' they say, 'Well I'm out there.' Now what is that crap?

**Hampton Hawes**

They're afraid to say it is nothing. There's no such thing as free form.

**Milt Jackson**

### FUSION AND ROCK:
## On the Corner

Frankly, to me, it's like the whole earth vomiting at once. The whole earth is sick, and it vomits. That to me is rock n' roll and discotheque dancing.

**Teddy Wilson**

I'm sorry to say that most players of my age, even some who are older, and of course those who are younger, just don't have a grip on the foundations; consequently, we're going to keep on having these monotonous one-chord vamps until they learn.

**Pat Metheny**

It was the hippest of times, it was the squarest of times, it was the spring of hope, it was the winter of despair.

**Leonard Feather on jazz
in the 1970s**

People think I'm trying to say jazz is greater than pop music. I don't have to say that, that's *obvious*.

**Wynton Marsalis**

The kids don't know why they go to the record shop and buy Elton John records. That's because they hear it all the time.
**Milt Jackson**

If you have personality it doesn't matter what you play anyhow. If you don't, there ain't no synthesizer in the world gonna help you or not any acoustic instrument either. It won't help you if you don't have it.
**Joe Zawinul**

We were the loudest band; we were louder even than the guys today with the amplifiers.
**Saxophonist Al Harding on the Stan Kenton Band**

Don't think about the fact that *Blood, Sweat & Tears* is currently the hottest rock album in the country. Pretend it's jazz.
**Columbia Records advertisement, 1969**

Take some chunka-chunka-chunka rhythm...you've got your 'groovin' formula and you stick with it interminably to create your 'magic'. But is it magic or just repetitious boredom?
*Downbeat* **Magazine review of Miles'** *On the Corner*, **1973**

John (McLaughlin) was really playing great, but he was getting very stoned, which was really saying something in those days. He actually fell off the stage at one gig in Coventry in an extremely stoned state and played this death chord as he landed...kkkkrrruuugggggg!
**Jack Bruce**

When I joined the band I didn't know any of the tunes, and when I left the band I didn't know the tunes!
**Keith Jarrett, on his stint with Miles Davis**

HERBIE HANCOCK: Well, Wynton is not an exponent of the idea that blending of musical cultures is a good thing.
WYNTON MARSALIS: Because it's an imitation of the root.

It loses roots because it's not a blending. It's like having sex with your daughter.
**Musician Magazine, March 1985**

I always had a secret desire to play on some of Sly Stone's records. I really wanted to do that for two years.
**Herbie Hancock**

The most intricate chord in the whole thing, I think, is a seventh.
**Ramsey Lewis on his recording "The 'In' Crowd"**

Because my name is associated with jazz, if I play two bars in the clear it's thought of as a jazz record.
**Herbie Hancock**

When we reach fusion, jazz is not trying to fuse anything into its sensibility, the jazz musician is trying to figure out how to fit into the sensibility of rock and roll so that it can make some money and get that audience.
**Stanley Crouch**

People like James Brown and Berry Gordy are much more meaningful to me, in my life, than a lot of so-called very big historical jazz figures. They have done more for black people.
**Donald Byrd**

I heard a test pressing that Walter (Becker) brought over. I put it on and thought, man, this is great. It's far too esoteric for the average pop buyer. It won't sell ten copies.
**Tom Scott on Steely Dan's album *Aja***

I would say that 75% of the time I was playing to some kind of metric, some kind of click. I just got tired of the process, it started getting clinical to me. In terms of production values I found myself sliding into that area and it felt very uncomfortable, like musical necrophilia, doing all the work and getting nothing back.
**David Sanborn**

### VOCALISTS:
# Sing Sing Sing

I don't understand the music, but I certainly understand the girl singer!
**Nikita Khrushchev to Benny Goodman during his Soviet tour**

She has the sort of large glowing voice, particularly bright in its upper reaches, that 30 years ago would have drawn her to "Michael, Row the Boat Ashore" and 10 years ago to *Cats*.
**Gary Giddins on Jane Monheit**

Doris Day was in the band when I joined in Chicago but she was just a girl vocalist and I wasn't interested in girl vocalists with any band; all I was interested in was the clarinet!
**Abe Most**

I've been called a blues singer and a jazz singer and a ballad singer—well, I'm all three, which means I'm just a singer.
**Helen Humes**

You're as good a singer as you sing your consonants. Without them, the words just don't end.
**Bobby Short**

I hate it when you can't understand the words. And I don't like nonsense music. The ones with two words: Get up and jump down.
**Etta Jones**

When I sing, I concentrate. I never think as I'm singing: Will lunch with Rex Reed tomorrow be canceled?
**Mel Torme**

Certain entertainers draw a certain element in audiences and in friends. If a singer sings a loser's love song, the audience identifies.
**Eddie Chamblee**

Q: Anita, what's your concept of your music?
Anita O'Day: It's according to how good or bad the coffee is.

I don't sing a lyric if I don't like it.  A song like "Feelings" is a bad lyric and a bad song.
**Billy Eckstine**

Ask any ten bandleaders as to their pet headache...nine will answer "girl vocalists"...yes, girl vocalists are a nuisance.
*Swing* **Magazine, 1938**

Bill (Basie) only liked to play in two keys, you know, and I don't sing in either one of them.
**Kay Starr**

Listen to the voice, don't *look* at her.
**Chick Webb on Ella Fitzgerald**

If you don't feel a thrill when Peggy Lee sings, you're dead, Jack.
**Leonard Feather**

Today's girl singers, poor kids, are the victims of a heritage of classic yodeling.
**Ted Toll, 1939**

I find it very insulting to be called an instrumental impersonator.
**Bobby McFerrin**

Bing (Crosby) was always kind and calm, but he was more given to living it up before he became an American institution.
**Hoagy Carmichael**

You know Bing, my lord, he couldn't walk across the street without an ad-lib.
**Dick Haymes**

And, I mean, the other thing in those days with the girl singers is you were cute and pert and jumped around a lot. And I hadn't been cute and pert since I was like six...

**Jo Stafford**

I always wanted to be a movie star. And look at this terrible thing that's happened to me now. I've become a singer!

**Mel Torme**

I don't care what you call me, as long as you give me a job.

**Dinah Washington**

The last six albums, seven albums I've made, I'm proud of. I really am. That doesn't mean that I get up in the morning and say "God, before I brush my teeth I gotta hear my golden voice." I never play my albums.

**Mel Torme**

Throw a banana peel out the window and your are sure to slip up a jazz singer in her/his 20s or 30s.

**Gary Giddins**

If you hear of anything new be sure and let me know—I wanna try it!

**Anita O'Day**

After me there are no more jazz singers

**Betty Carter**

I hate straight singing. I have to change a tune to my own way of doing it. That's all I know.

**Billie Holiday**

As for Billie Holiday, I don't know what to say about her. As far as I'm concerned, she is her worst enemy. She's a queer woman. She has a temperament.

**Carmen McRae**

Billie Holiday is a roly-poly young colored woman with a hump in her voice...She does not care enough about her figure to watch her diet, but she loves to sing.
**TIME Magazine**

There is no accounting for jazz singers, that is to say, singers who suffer from the dangerous delusion that they are jazz singers.
**Benny Green**

Ella knows her way around her voice as very few singers today.  But there are times when she seems to be unaware there are things a human voice just doesn't do.  She does them.
**Dom Cerulli on Ella Fitzgerald**

I like a good lyric that's not jumping into bed in the next line.  I like a lyric that means something, one that can be around 200 years from today.
**Etta Jones**

I have been sold out ever since that song has come out.  Everybody asks me the cliché question, "Don't you ever get tired of it?"  I always say to an interviewer, "Do *you* ever get tired of making love?" and it stops them cold.
**Tony Bennett on "I Left My Heart in San Francisco"**

Men like (James P. Johnson), Willie "The Lion" Smith, and Charlie Johnson could make you sing until your tonsils fell out.
**Ethel Waters**

### THE LATIN THING:
### La Fiesta

Stop telling stories.  Everyone knows it was Burt Bacharach who invented bossa nova.
**Dionne Warwick on a tour of Brazil, 1966**

# Quotable Jazz

With the money he earned from the Getz/Gilberto album...Stan Getz bought a home in Irvington, New York, that had belonged to Frances Gershwin, sister of the late George...For his participation in the record, Joao Gilberto, as co-star, received $23,000...Astrud Gilberto, who sang "Garato de Impanema" in English and was responsible for the record's international success earned what the American musicians' syndicate paid for a single night of work: $120.

**Ruy Castro, *Bossa Nova***

Anyone who says they went to America and made lots of money is lying.  Including me.

**Laurindo de Almeida**

Any person, I think, who digs jazz, will dig the mambo.

**Tito Puente**

In Portuguese, a *bossa* means a protuberance, a hump, a bump.  And the human brain has these protuberances—the bumps in the head...So if a guy has a *bossa* for something, it is literally a bump in the brain...

**Antonio Carlos Jobim**

When they start to play clave, that's Hispanic, Afro, Latin rhythms.  If a majority of the time your rhythm section is playing that, it's not jazz.  It's Afro-Hispanic music.

**Stanley Crouch**

## JAZZ POETRY:
## Wouldn't That Be Kerouac?

The author of the much–acclaimed novel, *On the Road*, lasted all of two performances.  His short run was due not to the fact that he didn't draw well, but rather that the large crowd of "beatniks" who appeared were either unable or unwilling to spend money. They came and listened, but forgot to order.

**Bob Rolontz on Jack Kerouac's appearance at NYC's Village Vanguard for a jazz poetry performance**

I hate the way Jack Kerouac writes. I kind of like the way he lives, though.
**Paul Desmond**

Jack Kerouac: I should have been a jazz musician. I would have been a great tenor saxophonist.

J.J. Johnston: No, I picture you more as a trumpeter.

It is doubtful if jazz poetry will receive much attention in the next encyclopedia of jazz.
**Bob Rolontz**

## Composers & Arrangers:
## I Could Write a Book

...That song was written really because it was a very hot day and we decided to cool ourselves off, and what came out was "Chestnuts Roasting on an Open Fire".
**Mel Torme**

I wrote "Lullaby of Birdland" in ten minutes over a steak in my dining room when I lived in New Jersey. I always say it took ten minutes to write and 35 years in the business, you know how that goes.
**George Shearing**

Fats Waller could turn out songs faster than he could remember them.
**Leonard Feather**

Bing (Crosby) didn't want a song that was mushy, so we never wrote any mushy love songs for him.
**Jimmy Van Huesen**

You should write music that's singable.
**Archie Shepp**

I remember when I first started writing for Basie, a fellow in the band said "Sammy, I heard Basie talkin' last night and he said, 'You know, the trouble with these young people that are always writin' for me, they want to write like Basie. They should write like themselves and we'll *play* it like Basie!'"

**Arranger Sammy Nestico**

I wish you wouldn't make the strings such an important part of your arrangements because frankly they're only a tax dodge!

**Tommy Dorsey to Nelson Riddle**

I'm anti-composition. We like to think of keeping the taxi waiting while we make the record, as opposed to spending three months in the studio.

**Paul Bley**

I cry a lot, and when I'm not doing that I roll around under the piano.

**Gerry Mulligan, on his compositional methods**

I don't need time. What I need is a deadline!

**Duke Ellington**

## DRUMMERS:
## The Main Man

I don't want no drummer. *I* set the tempo.

**Bessie Smith**

Krupa's drums went through us like a triple bourbon.

**Eddie Condon on Gene Krupa**

Gene had excitement. If he gained a little speed, so what? Better than sitting on your ass just getting by.

**Benny Goodman on Gene Krupa**

I enrolled in a conservatory, with a percussion major...Well, the first thing he said to me was that I held the sticks wrong.

Now I was on 52nd Street working with Charlie Parker, Coleman Hawkins, making more money than he was making...I said "Man, if I change the way I hold the sticks and everything, I wouldn't be able to pay my tuition to this place."
**Max Roach**

Every three beats a drummer plays, he owes Jo five.
**Max Roach on Jo Jones**

I learnt a long time ago, when you play drums for a person like Johnny Hodges, you are the accompaniment, he is the soloist. Sometimes today you get drummers who want to be soloists against the Johnny Hodgeses and it doesn't work.
**Louis Bellson**

You have guys like Buddy (Rich), Louis Bellson. These guys are like good wine. The older they become, the better they play.
**Henry Adler**

The people I didn't want to play with, I didn't play with. The places I didn't want to go, I didn't go. I'm like Elsa the lion, born free.
**Jo Jones**

Going to see Jonathan David Samuel Jones...is like entering a time warp inhabited by sand dancers, musicians, slapstick comedians, chorus girls, blues singers, and nomadic musical gladiators.
**Chip Stern on Jo Jones**

No drummer influenced me. Any time I saw a drummer, I knew what he was going to do after he had played two bars.
**Jo Jones**

I sleep with the door unlocked. I've never locked my door in my life. I don't fear anyone or anything.
I realize that personally, myself, I'm fifty people.
**Jo Jones**

### AT THE PIANO:
## The Pearls

The keyboard idea is one of the immense illusions in music at the moment. The keyboard is being used like a Parker Brothers game, a version of three-dimensional chess which they can sell to people who can't play two-dimensional chess.
**Keith Jarrett**

I despair about the lack of proper respect shown for the piano. If you want it to sound like a traffic jam, go out in the street and create a traffic jam and forget the piano. That's not a piano sound.
**Oscar Peterson**

Where are you going to stand when you play your trumpet, Mr. Peterson?
**Anonymous photographer to Oscar Peterson**

I don't like being called a jazz pianist, just the same way I'm not a blind pianist. I'm a pianist.
**George Shearing**

Many clubs pay more attention to their trashcans than the house piano.
**Bill Evans**

Learn to play the piano, man, and then you can figure out crazy solos of your own.
**Dizzy Gillespie to Miles Davis**

I can leave the piano for one week. It's like love. I can stay one week without, but when you make you make very well. It's like a man to me. But it's the piano that gives me this sensation. Not like a man who gives me when he wants to give me.
**Tania Maria**

## NAWLINS:
## Do You Know What It Means to Miss New Orleans

New Orleans is the only place I know of where you ask a little kid what he wants to be and instead of saying "I want to be a fireman" or "I want to be a policeman" he says "I want to be a musician"
**Alan Jaffe**

Yes, they danced absolutely stripped, but in New Orleans the naked dance was a real art.
**Jelly Roll Morton**

The word (jazz) never lost its association with those New Orleans bordellos. In the 1920s I used to try to convince Fletcher Henderson that we ought to call what we were doing "Negro music". But it's too late for that now.
**Duke Ellington**

New Orleans, until the 'twenties, was the safest haven in the Americas for the world's most vicious characters.
**Danny Barker**

I don't know if it was rough or not. I was rough right along with it.
**Billie Pierce on her start as a pianist
in the '20s in New Orleans**

In the matter of jass, New Orleans is particularly interested, since it has been widely suggested that this particular form of musical vice had its birth in this city...We do not recognize the honor of parenthood, but with such a story in circulation, it behooves us to be last to accept the atrocity in polite society...
**The *Times-Picayune* (New Orleans)**

New Orleans is now and has ever been the hoodoo capital of America.
**Zora Neale Hurston**

## New York, New York:
## Scrapple From The Apple

It ain't a bit hard to find someone who's lonesome or for-lorn here...But it's like finding a needle in a haystack to find somebody who was born here.
**Jon Hendricks, "New York, New York"**

I never heard of any such thing as a "New York sound". It's a funny thing...they have always kept any originality in jazz away from New York City...This place makes *all* musicians sound kind of funny when they come around. When they first come here, I don't care what they were in their hometowns, when they come *here* they get cut.
**Coleman Hawkins**

What (New York) seems to me is, like, a large record store that wants to stock everything that's been recorded. And, there-fore, they don't have any taste.
**Keith Jarrett**

I don't think I'm really ready for New York.
**Art Tatum, 1928**

Tell the New York cats to look out. Here comes Tatum! And I mean every living tub with the exception of Fats Waller and Willie the Lion.
**Art Tatum, 1930**

If you're living in the middle of nowhere you can live in a fantasy world of being someone else. In New York you have to find yourself really quick.
**Lew Tabackin**

Look, I was in New York before you got here. I'll be here when you're gone.
**Dizzy Gillespie to bassist Oscar Pettiford**

## Jazz Around the World:
## Le Jazz Hot

My feeling is, music is a more eloquent international language than Coca-Cola or McDonalds.
**Paul Horn**

American music, jazz music, must be played by men who were brought up to drink rye and Coke in juke joints. A lifetime of blond beer in Munich or Torino Vermouth isn't quite the same thing.
**Gene Krupa**

Jazz is known all over the world as an American musical art form and that's it. No America, no jazz. I've seen people try to connect it to other countries, for instance to Africa, but it doesn't have a damn thing to do with Africa.
**Art Blakey**

The Europeans at this point are ready to say, 'Hey,, guys, we'll take jazz from here. You don't know what the hell to do with it.'
**Quincy Jones**

The only things that the United States has given to the world are skyscrapers, jazz, and cocktails. That is all. And in Cuba, in our America, they make much better cocktails.
**Federico García Lorca**

It is veneer, rouge, aestheticism, art museums, new theaters, etc. that make America impotent. The good things are football, kindness, and jazz bands.
**George Satayana**

The music scene in Spain is like being nowhere, and playing nothing with nobody.
**Kai Winding**

# Quotable Jazz

Some people believe that English plumbing is to be reckoned among the four wonders of the world. They are wrong. Let them listen to what an English band imagines it is doing when it attempts to play jazz. Such a caterwauling was never heard anywhere else on this earth.

**Ashley Montagu**

It was evident that the further we go away from Manila, the staler the jazz. In Cairo we heard some of the new Sheik songs ground out this year in Tin Pan Alley, whereas in Japan—ten days from Seattle—they were still playing old songs. Japan really is the crossroads where jazz ends and ragtime begins.

**Burnet Hershey**

Those Scandinavian chicks are the cutest, and the cats are great. They are very warm people. Italy is crazy, and they have just about the sharpest gang of people anywhere, but they are not as down on swing as in some other countries. You can't play the Germans cheap, either, because they dig jazz in a nice, cool way. But Paris and London are the boss towns.

**Dicky Wells**

Today he plays jazz; tomorrow he betrays his country.

**Stalinist slogan in the Soviet Union (1920s)**

The building of Socialism proceeds more lightly and more rhythmically to the accompaniment of jazz.

**Polish government propaganda (1955)**

The hours we spent racking our brains over song titles we couldn't understand..."Struttin' With Some Barbecue"—the definition of the word "barbecue" in our pocket Webster didn't help at all. What on earth could it mean:"walking pompously with a piece of animal carcass roasted whole?"

**Josef Skvorecky**

In 1953 we crossed the Swiss border more times than a smuggler.

**Buddy Childers**

I didn't dare be seen on the street; people would rip my clothes off! I'd just run as fast as I could to get away from these people, and look for doorways to duck into.
**Stan Kenton, on touring Europe**

The audience applauded by stomping their feet. You had the feeling you were in Nazi Germany, striking a blow for democracy!
**Bill Russo on playing Berlin in 1953**

Man, I nearly got cheered to death.
**Trumpeter Rex Stuart on a concert in Berlin**

Daddy-O, it was the most.
**Ella Fitzgerald on a Jazz at the Philharmonic
performance in Sweden**

The English voted me the greatest singer in the world. So I stayed five years.
**Jon Hendricks**

We went to Vietnam eight years in a row from the time that silly Johnson sent people over there until it finally came to a stalemate around '72 or '73.
**Les Brown**

All of 'em.
**Louis Armstrong on his favorite European country**

I was supposed to play two concerts that night, but they broke up the chairs—they got tired of applaudin' with their hands and started applaudin' with the chairs...
**Louis Armstrong on a riot that broke out at a
concert in Hamburg in 1955**

In Europe they think we're abject idiots and uncultured beasts for ignoring our own culture.
**Jon Hendricks**

This music makes our job much easier.
**Donald Heath, U.S. Ambassador to Lebanon on
Dizzy Gillespie's Mideast tour, 1956**

I used to do a lot of apologizing for what the State Department had done.
**Dizzy Gillespie on his U.S. State Department-sponsored tours**

I don't need that kind of life just so I can work more often, drive on the left side of the road and walk free down a boulevard with a blonde bitch on my arm.
**Hampton Hawes on jazz musicians living in Europe**

## V. SOME OF THE GREATS

### Louis Armstrong:
### West End Blues

Armstrong: a high note or series of high notes played on a trumpet, especially in jazz.
***Dictionary of American Slang***

Who's to say that Louis Armstrong's soul was greater than anybody else's? How can you measure soul? Have any women left him, did he eat some chicken on Saturday night?
**Wynton Marsalis**

I mean, after all, how can you help loving a guy that makes the world smile and a happy place like Louis does? If he couldn't blow or sing a note, he'd still be worth his weight in laughs.
**Muggsy Spanier**

I have a friend that teaches literature at Santa Monica City College, and she asked the students to bring in a paper on Louis Armstrong. One of the girls, the first thing she said was, "Well, he was the first man on the moon."
**Harry "Sweets" Edison**

All music is folk music. I ain't never heard a horse sing a song.
**Louis Armstrong**

So many people died of trying to imitate Louis (Armstrong), sticking their heads out of windows in a blizzard. They died of choking, trying to get that raspy voice like Satchmo's.
**Danny Barker**

There is two kinds of music the good and bad. I play the good kind.
**Louis Armstrong**

### BENNY GOODMAN:
## Don't Be That Way

He would forget everybody's name so everybody was called Pops.
**Helen Forrest (on Benny Goodman)**

It got to the point where everybody was "Pops" to him—women, children, dogs, fire hydrants; everything was "Pops."
**Terry Gibbs on Benny Goodman**

As for Benny Goodman, well, in those days, he really didn't know what he wanted. He thought that there never was any money in jazz until much later when John Hammond came along and showed him.
**Bud Freeman**

Yeah, Benny was—boring. Everything was strictly business with Benny; there were no laughs and he never, never, never ceased to try out reeds.
**Dick Haymes on Benny Goodman**

Benny wasn't too cool. In fact, he was outright corny to me.
**Lee Konitz on Goodman's so-called "bop" band**

(Goodman) became famous (or notorious) for staring at a player he didn't like. It was called "the ray" by his men. You might perhaps call it "the death ray." Personally, I'm not sure if this was true or not. After all, it's very possible that he might have just been staring into space or thinking about the tempo of the next tune he was going to play.
**Teddy Wilson**

The old man gave me the ray and it stayed with me four days. I couldn't sleep.
**Ziggy Elman**

Oh, the ray—that was just bullshit. If you didn't look like a clarinet he didn't see you.
**Ruby Braff**

I'm quite open about it. I like to joke about it and say that Benny Goodman *drove* me to the Clinic!
**Marian McPartland on her brief stay at the Meninger Clinic
while she was playing for Benny Goodman**

Those people were mavericks. The only person who wanted them was me. I mean, was Gene Krupa hard to get? Was Bunny Berigan hard to get?
**Benny Goodman**

I've heard some of these Texas college bands, but they're on a different kick. They're strictly on a Stan Kenton-Count Basie kick. Not that there's anything wrong with that.
**Benny Goodman**

If playing bad notes all night is progressive music just call me the golden Bantam and leave me alone.
**Benny Goodman**

## Lester Young:
## Lester Leaps In

I'll always remember when I first heard Lester (Young). I'd never heard anyone like him before. He was a stylist with a different sound. A sound I'd never heard before or since. To be honest with you, I didn't much like it at first.
**Count Basie**

Lester had style—like the shape of a Coca-Cola bottle—or a Rolls Royce.
**Jo Jones**

In this country kings or dukes don't amount to nothing. The greatest man around then was Franklin D. Roosevelt, and he was the President so I started calling Lester The President. It got shortened to Pres.
**Billie Holiday on Lester Young**

Norman Granz never did let *me* make a record with no strings, you know. Charlie Yardbird made millions of records with strings and things...
**Lester Young**

Fletcher Henderson's wife would take me down to the basement where they had an old wind-up phonograph and she'd play me Coleman Hawkins records on it and she'd ask me: "Lester, can't you play like this?" Every morning that bitch'd wake me up at nine o'clock to teach me to play like Coleman Hawkins.
**Lester Young**

I remember the night Lester Young came (to *The Tonight Show*). He walked in...and I recognized the hat and the tenor case and stuff and I went right over to him and said "Lester, welcome; I'm Steve Allen." And he looked at me for a minute and then he moved up very close to me and in a very soft voice said, "Many eyes."

**Steve Allen**

It was at the Lincoln [Hotel] in New York in 1942 that Pres got his little bell. If somebody missed a note, or you were a new guy and goofed, you'd hear the bell going "ding-dong!" If Pres was blowing and goofed, somebody would reach over and ring his bell on him.

**Dicky Wells**

## BIRD:
# Ornithology

I'm no Bird, man! And Cannonball Adderley isn't either! Nobody's Bird! *Bird died!*

**Sonny Stitt**

Bird Lives!

**Unknown**

Bird's contribution to all the jazz that came after involved every phase of it. He sure wasn't the beginning, and he wasn't the end—but that middle was *bulging!*—

**Dizzy Gillespie**

After you play with Charlie Parker you don't have to worry about anything else. You've been through it.

**Dexter Gordon**

Bird made a blues out of 'Lady Be Good.' That solo made old men out of everyone on stage that night.

**John Lewis**

That horn ain't supposed to sound that fast.

**Ben Webster on Charlie Parker**

I owed Bird everything, but who could afford him?
**Anonymous**

Fan (to Dizzy): How's your dream band?
Dizzy: You mean my wet-dream band.
Bird (in a loud voice): Are you referring to somnambulistic ejaculation?

He looked like a used pork chop—so bad it was ridiculous. You never saw anything like him.  None of his clothes fit. His horn was all rubber bands and cellophane.
**Stan Levey on Charlie Parker**

A hostile, evasive personality with manifestations of primitive sexual fantasies associated with hostility and gross evidence of paranoid thinking.
**Bellevue psychiatric evaluation of Charlie Parker**

I didn't like whites walking into the club where we were playing just to see Bird act a fool, thinking he might do something stupid.
**Miles Davis on Charlie Parker**

Bird never excited me like he did the others.  'Bird is a god' they said.  He wasn't to me! No, and no one else was, either.
**Thelonious Monk**

Bird was the easiest of all musicians to record.  It was just a matter of getting him there.
**Ross Russell, owner of Dial Records**

Let's play the 'Star-Spangled Banner'; I think you can play that.
**Charlie Parker to an inept rhythm section**

When Bird came on the scene...it was just as shocking as in the Bible:  everything was dark, and then the light appeared for the first time.
**Shorty Rogers**

If Charlie Parker wanted to invoke plagiarism laws, he could sue almost everybody who's made a record in the last ten years.
**Lennie Tristano**

When Bird left New York he was a king, but out in Los Angeles he was just another broke, weird, drunken nigger playing some strange music.
**Miles Davis**

Civilization is a damn good thing, if somebody would try it.
**Charlie Parker**

You mean there is not a statue of Charlie Parker in Times Square?
**Danish tourist to writer Nat Hentoff**

(Charlie Parker) and I were like two peas...our music was like putting whipped cream on jello.
**Dizzy Gillespie**

I never thought I'd live to see 1955
**Charlie Parker**

Parker died on March 12, 1955

## MONK:
## Misterioso

The Monk runs deep.
**Charlie Parker**

Monk's not here!!
**The way Thelonious Monk often answered his telephone**

You gotta dig Thelonious as the thinker, the skull, the long medulla.
**Albert Goldman**

I dig to play Monk because Monk's tunes make you improvise on melody and not on chords. They have you thinking without thinking, like some kind of conscious unconscious. Or something.

**Don Cherry**

Monk may be a great aesthetic chef, but he is not a waiter: He may cook the food, but you have to get up and serve yourself.

**Stanley Crouch**

You're very much left to your own devices, you know, playing Monk's music with Monk accompanying...I mean, trying to express yourself because his music, with him comping, is so overwhelming, like it's almost like you're trying to break out of a room made of marshmallows.

**Johnny Griffin**

I say, play your own way. Don't play what the public wants. You play what you want and let the public pick up on what you're doing - even if it does take them fifteen, twenty years.

**Thelonious Monk**

They wanted me to pose in a monk's habit, on a pulpit, holding a glass of whiskey. I told them no. Monks don't even stand in pulpits.

**Thelonious Monk on a disagreement with Riverside Records
for the cover of his *Monk's Music* album**

Monk was a gentle person, gentle and beautiful, but he was strong as an ox. And if I had ever said something about punching Monk out in front of his face—and I never did—then somebody should have just come and got me and taken me to the madhouse, because Monk could have just picked my little ass up and thrown me through a wall.

**Miles Davis**

## BUDDY RICH:
# Big Band Machine

That damn fool knows the instrument.
**Jo Jones**

The people who play, will continue to play, and the people who steal and copy will continue to be bad imitations and thieves.
**Buddy Rich**

Get your foot the hell off my stage.
**Buddy Rich to an audience member**

If you have any requests, forget 'em. This is my band, and I'll play what I want.
**Buddy Rich**

I don't play as well as I want to play. And I'm a bitch!
**Buddy Rich**

Buddy's mellowed now—most people get that way if they live long enough. A couple of heart attacks give you a little pause.
**Nelson Riddle on Buddy Rich**

You must be from Boise, Idaho, man. The big swinger from Boise, in the big city for his once-a-year big night on the big jazz scene. Stand up, man, so everybody can see what a real jazz critic from Boise looks like.
**Buddy Rich to a heckler at Mr. Kelly's in Chicago**

I'm accustomed to working with number one musicians. I'm NOT accustomed to working with half-assed kids who think they wrote the fuckin' music business.
**Buddy Rich to a member of his band**

The doctors asked him if he was allergic to anything. Buddy said, "country and western music."
**Freddie Gruber on Buddy Rich**

The only two forms of music in any field are good and bad. What happens in between is up to the taste of Middle America, which has no taste at all, whether it be in politics or music.
**Buddy Rich**

I'll cancel the whole tour. I'll tell them to stick the tour up their ass. Nobody tells me who I can have in my band.
**Buddy Rich on playing in South Africa
with a racially mixed band**

### TRANE:
## Ascension
Most kids talk about John Coltrane, but Trane was very confused. I remember once when I opened at the Apollo Theatre, and it was packed, Coltrane was on the bill, playing all those little things he played, and he got hung up on a passage, and he kept playing that passage for half an hour. When I looked around, everybody was out of the theatre.
**Lionel Hampton**

It was almost superhuman, and the amount of energy he was using could have powered a space ship.
**Ira Gitler on John Coltrane**

Sometimes I'd think I was making music through the wrong end of a magnifying glass.
**John Coltrane**

He played quite a few solos back then that hippies-in-the-street began to hum. I challenge them to hum some of his solos now.
**Cannonball Adderley**

I'm into scales right now.
**John Coltrane**

Well, I ain't never heard no blues played like that!
**Cannonball Adderley on hearing Coltrane**

## Ornette Coleman:
## Dancing In Your Head

The day I met Ornette, it was about 90 degrees and he had on an overcoat. I was scared of him.
**Don Cherry**

I listened to him all kinds of ways. I listened to him high and I listened to him cold sober. I even played with him. I think he's jiving, baby. He's putting everybody on.
**Roy Eldridge**

Later, half a dozen good ole boys show Coleman how they feel about this new-fangled New York music down here in Baton Rouge. They beat him to the ground, kick him unconscious and bust his saxophone.
**M. Oldfield, *The Guardian Weekend***

Just say I think he needs seasoning. A lot of seasoning.
**Coleman Hawkins**

If Coltrane "progressed from" (i.e., was more horrible than) Parker, who but Ornette Coleman has progressed from Coltrane?
**Philip Larkin**

Hell, just listen to what he writes and how he plays. If you're talking psychologically, the man is all screwed up inside.
**Miles Davis**

## Miles Davis:
## Miles Runs The Voodoo Down

As long as I've been playing, they never say I done anything. They always say that some white guy did it.
**Miles Davis**

A legend is an old man with a cane known for what he used to do. I'm still doing it.
**Miles Davis**

When you're creating your own shit, man, even the sky ain't the limit.
**Miles Davis**

If they act too hip, you know they can't play shit.
**Miles Davis**

That's got to be Eric Dolphy—nobody else could sound that bad! The next time I see him I'm going to step on his foot. You print that. I think he's ridiculous. He's a sad motherfucker.
**Miles Davis,** *Downbeat* **Magazine blindfold test**

Those songs to me don't exist, you know? "So What" or *Kind of Blue*, I'm not going to play that shit...Those things are there. They were done in that era, the right hour, the right day, and it happened. It's over, it's on the record.
**Miles Davis**

(White people) don't want to have to admit that a black person could be doing something that they don't know about...so they run around talking about how great it is until the next "new thing" comes along.
**Miles Davis**

I didn't even go to listen to most jazz groups anymore, because they were only playing the same musical licks that we

played way back with Bird, over and over again; that, along with some of the things that Coltrane introduced, and maybe Ornette. It was boring to hear that shit.
**Miles Davis**

Keith played so nice I had to give him two pianos. I'd say, "Keith, how does it feel to be a genius?"
**Miles Davis on Keith Jarrett**

Miles is never wrong. But there's always more to say about it.
**Keith Jarrett**

I was getting too high and he said so. He said to cool out. And when Miles Davis tells you that you gotta realize that something must be wrong.
**Mike Stern**

I wish I was blacker. I'd like to be as black as you are, Miles.
**Bud Powell to Miles Davis**

In Europe, they like everything you do. The mistakes and everything. That's a little bit too much.
**Miles Davis**

I never thought that the music called "jazz" was ever meant to reach just a small group of people, or become a museum thing locked under glass like all other dead things that were once considered artistic.
**Miles Davis**

I really liked Wynton when I first met him. He's still a nice young man, only confused.
**Miles Davis on Wynton Marsalis**

Look, I wouldn't care if he came up on the bandstand in his B.V.D.'s and with one arm, just so long as he was there.
**Miles Davis on Philly Joe Jones**

I'm a John Lewis fan, and I like all of them, but I don't go with this bringing "dignity" to jazz. The way they bring "dignity" to jazz in their formal clothes and the way they bow is like Ray Robinson bringing dignity to boxing by fighting in a tuxedo.

**Miles Davis on the Modern Jazz Quartet**

That's what fucked up music, you know. Record companies. They make too many sad records, man.

**Miles Davis**

Producer,Teo Macero: OK, is this going to be Part 2?

Miles: It's gonna be Part 9...what difference does it make what the fuck part it is...

Macero: Alright, alright.

***Bitches Brew* recording seessions**

People who only followed him in his *Sketches of Spain* days, then didn't buy another album for a while, will be shocked when they hear what he's into now.  But I would rather see somebody experiment and fall on his ass than simply stagnate.

**Sammy Davis, Jr.**

There used to be a period when if a woman started becoming insecure when she got to be about forty, forty-five, you know, the top of the dress would get lower and the bottom of the dress would get higher and then she would end up, you know, going to discos and stuff...because she was trying to battle time.  Now I think Miles Davis, that's what happened to him, too.

**Stanley Crouch**

Miles was a soul man, a sound, a black Bogey.  He was also an insufferable prick.

**Albert Goldman**

How do I know why Miles walks off the stage? Why don't you ask him? And besides, maybe we'd all like to be like Miles, and just haven't got the guts.

**Dizzy Gillespie**

**Quotable Jazz**

It took me twenty years study and practice to work up to what I wanted to play in this performance. How can she expect to listen five minutes and understand it?
**Miles Davis on an audience member who complained that she didn't "understand" what he was playing**

Another bitch. A different brew. Get Up With It.
**Columbia advertisement for Miles' album *Get Up With It*, 1975**

Miles got a mystique about him—plus he's at the top of his profession. And he's got way, way, *way* more money.
**Dizzy Gillespie**

When the kids turn on their television sets, they want to see a Michael Jackson. And if it's a Miles Davis, he damn well better look something like a Michael Jackson.
**Archie Shepp**

## VI. FINAL THOUGHTS

### The Future of Jazz:
### The Shape of Jazz to Come

So look up all you cats, and get ready to leave the old milk and cracker diet, for the good old days are coming back.
***Downbeat* Magazine, February 1936**

I don't know where jazz is going. Maybe it's going to hell. You can't make anything go anywhere. It just happens.
**Thelonious Monk**

Jazz will endure just as long as people hear it with their feet instead of their brains.
**John Philip Sousa**

Jazz became many things—frenetic, destructive, hysterical, decadent, venal, alcoholic, saccharine, Lombardish, vapid...
**Alan Lomax**

116

What you're hearing these days is black magic, exercises, foreign sounds, rock, and free. You're not hearing jazz.
**Mary Lou Williams**

You know the actor John Garfield? In one movie he walked up to this train station, the ticket booth, and the guy says, 'Yes, where are you going?' And he says, 'I want a ticket to nowhere.' I thought: that's it. The freedom to do that. I want a ticket to nowhere.
**Wayne Shorter**

Jazz as we know it is dead.
***Downbeat* Magazine cover, 1967**

Jazz is dead, baby, ain't you glad?
**Charles Mingus**

I don't know what *I'm* going to do next, much less where jazz is going to go.
**Sonny Rollins**

I still claim that jazz hasn't gotten to its peak as yet. I may be the only perfect specimen today in jazz that's living. I guess I am 100 years ahead of my time. Jazz is a style, not a type of composition.
**Jelly Roll Morton**

Many people think that the world should speak the same language eventually...and many people think that would be a really good thing to happen. But I don't agree. If that was the way the earth was two hundred years ago, we would have no jazz. We would have no folk music to listen to from anywhere else. We would only have one thing, it would be like New Age music forever.

**Keith Jarrett**

Hell, nobody knows where jazz is really going to go. There may be a kid right now in Chitling Switch, Georgia, who's going to come along and upset everybody.

**Quincy Jones**

One of the things I like about jazz, kid, is I don't know what's going to happen next. Do you?

**Bix Beiderbecke**

## CODA

Let my children have music! Let them hear live music. Not noise. *My* children! You do what you want with your own.

**Charles Mingus**

May you all live to be four hundred years old and may the last voice you hear be mine.

**Frank Sinatra**

Everything was mostly fun, the whole thing!

**Count Basie**

# Index

# Bibliography

Frank Alkyer, *Downbeat: 60 Years of Jazz* (Hal Leonard, 1995)

Whitney Balliett, *Jelly Roll, Jabbo & Fats* (OxfordUniversity Press, 1983)

Count Basie as told to Albert Murray, *Good Morning Blues: The Autobiography of Count Basie* (Da Capo, 1985)

Sidney Bechet, *Treat It Gentle* (Da Capo, 1978)

Joshua Berrett, *The Louis Armstrong Companion* (Schirmer, 1999)

Hoagy Carmichael, *The Stardust Road and Sometimes I Wonder* (Da Capo, 1999)

Gary Carner, *Miles Davis Companion* (Music Sales Corp, 2000)

Dom Cerulli, et al, *The Jazz Word* (Da Capo, 1960)

James Lincoln Collier, *Benny Goodman and the Swing Era* (OxfordUniversity Press, 1989)

Mervyn Cooke, *The Chronicle of Jazz* (Abbeville Press, 1997)

Bill Crow, *From Birdland to Broadway: Scenes From a Jazz Life* (Oxford University Press, 1992)

Vince Danca, *2001 Compleat Jazz Calendar*

Stanley Dance, *The World of Count Basie* (Charles Scribners Sons, 1980)

Stanley Dance, *The World of Swing* (Da Capo, 1974)

Francis Davis, *Bebop & Nothingness* (Schirmer, 2000)

Scott DeVeaux, *The Birth of Bebop* (University of California Press, 1997)

Carol Easton, *Straight Ahead: The Story of Stan Kenton* (William Morrow & Co, 1973)

Duke Ellington, *Music Is My Mistress* (Da Capo, 1973)

*Esquire's 1947 Jazz Book* (Hearst Corporation, 1947)

Wane Ernstine, *Jazz Spoken Here* (Da Capo, 1994)

Leonard Feather, *The Passion for Jazz* (Da Capo, 1980)

Benny Green, *Drums in my Ears* (Davis Poynter Ltd, 1973)

Gary Giddins, *Riding on a Blue Note: Jazz and American Pop* (Oxford University Press, 1981)

Ted Gioia, *West Coast Jazz* (University of California Press, 1992)

Joe Goldbert, *Jazz Masters of the 50s* (Da Capo, 1965)

Robert Gottlieb *Reading Jazz* (Vintage Books, 1999)

Leslie Gourse, *Louis' Children: American Jazz Singers* (Cooper Square Press, 2001)

Fred Hall, *More Dialogues in Swing* (Pathfinder Publishing, 1991)

Hampton Hawes, *Raise Up Off Me* (Coward, McCann, and Geoghegan, Inc., 1972)

Nat Hentoff, *Jazz Is* (Limelight Editions, 1984)

Nat Hentoff, *Listen to the Stories* (Da Capo, 1995)

Zora Neal Hurston, *Mules and Men* (Lippincott, 1935)

Rick Kennedy and Randy McNutt, *Little Labels—Big Sound* (Indiana University Press, 1999)

Burt Korall, *Drummin' Men, The Hearbeat of Jazz* (Schirmer, 1990)

Philip Larkin, *All What Jazz: A Record Diary, 1961-1971* (Farrar, Straus, Giroux, 1985)

Philip Larkin, *Selected Letters of Philip Larkin 1940-1995* (Faber & Faber, 1992)

Gene Lees, *Cats of Any Color* (Da Capo, 1995)

Gene Lees, *Oscar Peterson: The Will to Swing* (Prima Publishing, 1990)

Gene Lees, *You Can't Steal a Gift* (Yale University Press, 2001)

James Lester, *Too Marvelous for Words: The Life and Genius of Art Tatum* (Oxford University Press, 1994)

Graham Lock, *Forces in Motion:  Anthony Braxton and the Meta-Reality of Creative Music* (Quartet, 1988)

Len Lyons, *The Great Jazz Pianists* (Quill, 1983)

Ashley Montague, *The American Way of Life* (G. P. Putnam & Sons, 1967)

Lewis MacAdams, *Birth of the Cool* (Free Press, 2001)

Donald L. Maggin, *Stan Getz: A Life in Jazz* (William Morrow & C, 1996)

David Margolick, *Strange Fruit: The Autobiography of a Song* (Eco Press, 2001)

Wynton Marsalis and Carl Vigeland, *Jazz in the Bitterseet Blues of Life* (Da Capo, 2001)

Kenny Mathieson, *Giant Steps: Bebop & the Creators of Modern Jazz 1945-65* (Payback Press, 1999)

David Meltzer, *Writing Jazz* (Mercury House, 1999)

Eric Olsen, et al, *The Encylclopedia of Record Producers* (Watson Guptill, 1999)

Richard Palmer, *Oscar Peterson* (Hippocrene Books, 1984)

Peter Pettinger, *Bill Evans: How My Heart Sings* (Yale, 1998)

Doug Ramsey, *Jazz Matters: Reflections on The Music and Some of Its Makers* (University of Arkansas Press, 1989)

Robert George Reisner, *Bird*: The legend of Charlie Parker (Da Capo, 1975)

Ross Russell, *Bird Lives: The High Life and Hard Times of Charlie (Yardbird) Parker,* (Da Capo, 1973)

Gene Santoro, *Myself When I Am Real* (Oxford University Press, 2000)

Winthrop Sargeant, *Jazz, Hot and Hybrid* (Da Capo, 1975)

Artie Shaw, *The Trouble With Cinderella* (Da Capo, 1979)

Ben Sidran, *Talking Jazz: An Oral History* (Da Capo, 1995)

David D. Spitzer, *Jazz* (Woodford Press, 1994)

Marshall W. Stearns, *The Story of Jazz* (Oxford University Press, 1956)

W. Royal Stokes, *The Jazz Scene* (Oxford University Press, 1991)

John F. Szwed, *Space Is the Place: The Lives and Times of Sun Ra,* (Pantheon, 1997)

Sheila Tracy, *Bands, Booze and Broads* (Mainstream Publishing Co. Ltd, 1995)

Frederick Turner, *Remembering Song* (Da Capo, 1994)

Dicky Wells as told to Stanley Dance, *Night People* (Smithsonian Press, 1991)

Martin Williams, *Jazz Changes* (Oxford University Press, 1992)

Teddy Wilson with Arie Ligthart and Humphrey Van Loo, *Teddy Wilson Talks Jazz* (Cassell, 1996)

Bill Zehme, *The Way You Wear Your Hat: Frank Sinatra and the Lost Art of Livin'* (Harper Collins, 1997)

## Periodicals:

*Antaeus*
*Army Times*
*Atlantic Monthly*
*Christian Science Monitor*
*Downbeat*
*Jazztalk*
*JazzTimes*
*Ladies Home Journal*
*Melody Maker*
*Metronome*
*Music*
*Musician*
*New Orleans Times-Picayune*
*New York Times*
*New York Times Sunday Magazine*
*Newsweek*
*Playboy*
*Rolling Stone*
*Soho Weekly News*
*The Etude*
*The Guardian*
*Tops*
*Village Voice*
*Wall Street Journal*

## Online

jazzitude.com
allaboutjazz.com
jazzinstituteofchicargo.org

# Recordings

*Thelonious Monk At the Five Spot*, Thelonious Monk, Milestone
  M-47043 liner notes by Stanley Crouch
*Best of Ella Fitzgerald*, Decca Records DXB-156 liner notes by
  Dom Cerulli
*The Blues*, Big Bill Broonzy, EmArcy Records MG 36137 liner
  notes by Studs Terkel
*The Complete Bitches' Brew Sessions*, Miles Davis, Columbia
  Records
*Kansas City Revisited*, Bob Brookmeyer, United Artists Records
  LP UA-5008 liner notes by Bob Brookmeyer
*The Lester Young Story*, Vol. 1, Columbia CG 33502
*Let My Children Hear Music*, Charles Mingus, Columbia
  KC 31039 liner notes by Charles Mingus
*Lil Armstrong: Satchmo and Me*, Riverside
  RLP 12-120 liner notes by Lil Armstrong
*Ornette Coleman, The Complete Atlantic Recordings*,
  Rhino Atlantic Jazz
*Relaxin' With The Miles Davis Quintet*, Miles Davis,
  Prestige Records
*Stan Getz: The Girl From Impanema: The Verve Bossa Years*,
  Stan Getz, Verve, 1989 liner notes by Neil Tesser

## The Editor

Marshall Bowden is a freelance writer and web designer who lives in Chicago, Illinois. He runs the independent jazz site Jazzitude at www.jazzitude.com. In addition, Mr. Bowden has contributed to *PopMatters*, where he writes reviews and a column, *All About Jazz.com*, where he writes the "Late Night Thoughts On Jazz" column, *Chicago Jazz Magazine*, and *transistornet* where he discusses rock and pop music.

Marshall has studied music for much of his life, studying classical piano from the age of eight and taking up alto sax at age ten. He quickly became interested in jazz, and played keyboards, alto and baritone sax in jazz bands and ensembles through high school. Along the way he picked up bassoon for the school orchestra, began learning clarinet, and studied arranging. He attended Berklee College of Music, later transferring to Washington University in St. Louis where he majored in English Literature. He spent several years working in the publishing industry and earned an MBA from DePaul University in Chicago in 2001.

## The Illustrator

Mike Rooth is a graduate of Sheridan College's Interpretive Illustration program, the last class of the 20th century. A St. Catharines native, he now lives in Oakville, Ontario, where he works as a freelance illustrator. Over the past two years his work has appeared in a wide variety of publications, both local and international. This is his second Sound And Vision book.

First published in Canada by
**Sound And Vision**
359 Riverdale Avenue
Toronto, Canada, M4J 1A4
www.soundandvision.com

First printing, September 2002
1 3 5 7 9 - printings - 10 8 6 4 2

---

**National Library of Canada Cataloguing in Publication**

Quotable jazz: by Marshall Bowden.
Caricatures by Mike Rooth.
Includes index.
ISBN 0-920151-55-8

1. Jazz—Quotations, maxims, etc.  I. Bowden, Marshall  II.
Rooth, Mike  III. Series.
ML3506.Q92 2002     781.65     C2002-904223-2

---

Typset in ITC Officinia
Printed and bound in Canada

# Other Quotable Books

## Quotable Pop
Fifty Decades of Blah Blah Blah
Compiled & Edited by Phil Dellio & Scott Woods
Caricatures by Mike Rooth
isbn 0-920151-50-7

## Quotable Opera
Compiled & Edited by Steve & Nancy Tanner
Caricatures by Umberto Tàccola
isbn 0-920151-54-X

## Quotable Alice
Compiled & Edited by David W. Barber
Illustrations by Sir John Tenniel
isbn 0-920151-52-3

## Quotable Sherlock
Compiled & Edited by David W. Barber
Illustrations by Sidney Paget
isbn 0-920151-53-1

## Quotable Twain
Compiled & Edited by David W. Barber
isbn 0-920151-56-6

## Note from the Publisher

Sound And Vision books may be purchased for educational or promotional use or for special sales. If you have any comments on this book or any other books we publish, or if you would like a catalogue, please write to us at Sound And Vision 359 Riverdale Avenue, Toronto, Canada M4J 1A4.

We are always looking for original books to publish. If you have an idea or manuscript that is in the genre of musical humour including educational themes, please contact us. Thank you for purchasing or borrowing this book.

Please visit our web site at http://www.soundandvision.com.

Geoff Savage
*Publisher*